James Thompson Bixby

Religion and Science As Allies

Or, similarities of physical and religious knowledge. Vol. 1

James Thompson Bixby

Religion and Science As Allies

Or, similarities of physical and religious knowledge. Vol. 1

ISBN/EAN: 9783337248413

Printed in Europe, USA, Canada, Australia, Japan

Cover: Foto ©Lupo / pixelio.de

More available books at **www.hansebooks.com**

RELIGION AND SCIENCE

AS

ALLIES

OR

SIMILARITIES OF PHYSICAL AND RELIGIOUS KNOWLEDGE

BY

JAMES THOMPSON BIXBY

CHICAGO
CHARLES H. KERR & COMPANY
175 DEARBORN STREET
1889

"Science was Faith once; Faith were Science now
Would she but lay her bow and arrow by,
And arm her with the weapons of the time."

"In vain would the skeptic make a distinction between science and common life, or between one science and another. The arguments employed in all, if just, are of a similar nature and contain the same force and evidence. Or, if there be any difference among them, the advantage lies entirely on the side of theology and natural religion."—CLEANTHES, IN HUME'S "DIALOGUES," Part I.

CONTENTS.

CHAPTER IV.

CHAPTER V.

CHAPTER VI.

CHAPTER VII.

CHAPTER VIII.

PHYSICAL AND RELIGIOUS KNOWLEDGE.

INTRODUCTION.

THE conflict now going on between the physical discoveries and theories of these latter days, and the forms of faith which have hitherto ruled the mind of Christendom, is one of the most noticeable phenomena of the intellectual movement of the times. The constant discussions from pulpit and platform, the numerous essays, pamphlets, and books, in which these two opponents are arrayed one against the other, and attack, defense, or effort at reconciliation made, allow no intelligent man or woman to remain unaware of the controversy.

It is a fact, so notorious that we need specify no particular instances nor details, that, by a large part of the Church, modern science is looked upon as a godless and blind teacher, a sacrilegious intruder upon the domain of revealed truth, and that, among almost all denominations and phases of religious thought, there has been more or less suspicion, jealousy, and abuse of physical investigation. It is a fact almost equally patent that, on the part of science likewise, among many, at least, of its representatives, there is a similar hostility entertained toward religion, and that not only all ecclesiastical organizations, but all spiritual faith and principles, are looked upon as their natural foes.

Now, this present antagonism of religion and science is a matter which may justly give concern, I believe, to all who have at heart the welfare of either. It is becoming quite plain to all clear-sighted observers that religion certainly cannot afford the continuance of any such quarrel.

"The problem of our age," said Archdeacon Hare, in his life of Sterling, "is to reconcile faith with knowledge, philosophy with religion. The men of our age will not believe unless you prove to them that what they are called upon to believe does not contradict the laws of their minds, and that it rests upon a solid and unshaken foundation."

In former conflicts, the struggle had been to preserve the Church from division, or the orthodox doctrine from aberrations or perversions.

In the present controversy, the debate concerns the fundamental ideas of religion. Twenty-five years ago Dr. Newman said to a sectarian controversialist, "Let us discuss the prospects of Christianity itself, instead of the differences between Anglican and Catholic." To-day such a change of front is still more necessary. More than ever before it is the citadel of Christianity, rather than her outposts, that needs to be defended. The wise Christian will turn his arms from these petty skirmishes about tapers and genuflexions, millinery of priests and wording of creeds, the sense of Hebrew numerals and the supernatural efficacy of drops of water, to ward off the blows of a nearer enemy—an invader who is pushing his way already with uplifted battle-axe into the Holy of Holies.

In former assaults upon religion, it was cynics, and worldlings, and doubters of every thing, who led the attack. Jest and jibe, scoff and sneer, were the favorite weapons of attack. Believers had only to stand firm in courage and patience on the unassailed foundations of their faith, and the strong currents of man's instinctive yearnings would before long turn the tide of popular opinion the other way, and bring the Church safely through its peril. To-day, however, the objections presented against religion are brought forward in no frivolous spirit, from no mere feverish mental excitability or love of innovation, but in the sincerity of an earnest loyalty to truth, out of a serious desire to get at the reality of things, through all illusions and at all risks. It is not ridicule, but reason, that leads the assault. The weapons are not the clown's bells and grinning mask, but the astronomer's spectroscope, the biologist's flask. The scales in which Christianity would now be tested are not those of universal skepticism, but of cautious, critical weighing of historic evidence and scientific proof. This method, of course, is a slower one than that of the French encyclopedists. Religion has not to fear that any such rapid and radical revolution can now occur in the belief of Christendom as was wrought in France in the last quarter of the eighteenth century. But it is a much more dangerous course to its adversary. The ground it gains it keeps. Like an Alpine glacier, its slow, gigantic plane grinds to powder the most flinty obstructions, and never loses a foot of ground that it has once taken. For four hundred years Science has driven the Church from post to post. The sphericity or the flatness of the earth, the mobility or stationariness of the globe, the six days' creation, the six thousand years' age of the world and of man, the universal deluge—these all have been battle-fields where the scientist and the ecclesiastic have met in conflict, and in every engagement it has been the ecclesiastic that has been worsted, and the scientist that has been victorious. The result is, that science to-day holds such a position that the belief of the next century may be said to lie in its hands. The facts that its distinguished *savans* establish to-day, in six months will be read in every newspaper and magazine in the civilized world; in ten years will be incorporated in our school-books, and planted in the forming minds of our children; in thirty years will be the creed of every educated man; and, before a century has passed, will be the universal belief of all classes. If Christianity cannot harmonize nerself with science, it is much to be feared that the fate of the Ptolemaic system of the universe will, at no very distant period, be hers ; at least, no one can doubt that the future of Religion would be vastly more sure and prosperous if she could make science an ally instead of a rival.

Nor for science, either, is it a matter of indifference what its relation toward religion is. While science stands, or is believed to stand, in an attitude of hostility to religion, it carries an unnecessary burden, which impedes no little its progress. The antagonism, whether it be real or only supposed, weakens its power and circumscribes its sphere of influence. It diverts its attention from its proper work to uncalled-for polemics. It vitiates the impartiality of judgment and equanimity of temperament which are required of it. Moreover, it is only, I venture to say, when science can gain the inspiration of the religious spirit, and be led forward and upward by such a conviction as animated Kepler, that, in tracing out the laws of Nature, he was thinking God's thoughts after him—it is only when pursued in this mood, I believe, that science can do its best work.

To bring, then, these two poles of modern thought into harmonious relations with each other, is a work of prime importance. On it depend the integrity and coördination of those two factors of man's higher existence—the aspirations of his soul and the perceptions of his intellect—for whose development all

other things are but instrumentalities.   It is one of
those questions that cannot be discussed too much.
It may be worn threadbare, but it cannot be shoved
out of sight.   The multitude of writings and publi-
cations concerning it but show how profound and
universal is the interest in it.   It is because of this
interest that I venture to contribute a few thoughts,
designed, if possible, to clear up some of the complications and remove some of the oppositions of the
controversy.   My purpose is not, I wish it to be
understood, to smooth over any real difficulties, to
bridge any natural hiatuses, or to accommodate or
compromise any inherent antagonisms.   Such work
is always, I believe, useless, if not mischievous.   Nor
is it to do, what so many have essayed, to show de-
tailed coincidences or particular correspondences between the present results of science and the testimony of the Scriptures; to demonstrate how the six
days of creation answer to the epochs of modern
geology; to exhibit the agreement of ethnography
with mankind's descent from a single couple; to
illustrate by modern hygiene the wisdom of the Le-
vitical regulations; or to disclose, in expressions of
Job, or David, or Isaiah, anticipations of modern
discoveries.   A flexile and ingenious interpreter, not
over-scrupulous about twisting words and forcing
facts, can always do this.   As Prof. Huxley has
said, "One never knows what exegetic ingenuity
may make of the original Hebrew."   In that grand
storehouse of thought and imagination, that vener-

able encyclopædia of all the poetry, science, history, and philosophy, in which the Jewish mind flowered under the inspiration of the Spirit of God, in that Bible whose original and proper name, we should al- ways remember, is, *the Books* (τα βιβλια), not the *Book*—in that grand storehouse it is always pos- sible to find plenty of parallels, more or less strong, for almost every conceivable notion. Each past generation has found there its favorite theories: in Tertullian's age, the materiality of the soul; in Au- gustine's, the flatness of the earth; in the time of the schoolmen, the Aristotelian philosophy: fifty years ago, the cataclysmal systems of geology, the Cuvierian distinction of species, the creation from the dust and primitive enlightenment of man by di- rect exertion of supernatural power; to-day, it is but little more difficult to find in the same pages author- ity or allowance for the nebular hypothesis, the evo- lution theory, and the savage if not animal origin of civilized man;[1] to-morrow, again, the same method of interpretation may show the coincidence of the Scriptures with whatever newer discovery Science may have made, or imagined that she has made. The

[1] The Rev. Mr. Mahin, for instance, in a communication to THE POPULAR SCIENCE MONTHLY, p. 487, August, 1875, says: "Even the modern doctrine of evolution—Darwinism, if you please—is as nearly taught in the first chapter of Genesis as in the revelations of modern science; and spontaneous generation seems to appear on the very face of the statements of Moses as therein recorded. Read verses 20 and 24: 'And God said, Let *the waters bring forth abundantly*,' etc. 'And God said, Let the *earth bring forth*,' etc."

hunting up of such correspondences is of very little value for any permanent reconciliation between science and religion.   As the Dean of Canterbury, Dr. Payne Smith, has well said,[1] " If the wisest geologist of our days could show that there was an exact agreement between geology and the Bible, it would rather disprove than prove its truth.   For, as geology is a growing science, it would prove the agreement of the Bible with that which is receiving daily additions, and is constantly undergoing modification, and ten years hence the two would be at hopeless variance."   The closer the coincidence happens to be shown in this present hour, the sooner it is likely disagreement will be revealed by the advancement of science, and the present interpretation of the sacred text become obsolete and require revision.   The continual varying of her interpretation, and shifting of her ground, to which Religion is necessitated, when by this method it seeks reconciliation with physical knowledge, inevitably throws discredit upon her. It makes Faith appear as a defendant, continually obliged to Science for permission to live ; as a satellite reflecting the varying phases of the scientific primary, rather than as an independent power—the central, self-subsistent Sun of Righteousness.

My aim, then, contemplates none of these objects or methods.   It is, instead, looking at religion and science in their broadest and most essential features,

---

[1] P. 175, " Modern Skepticism," Lectures of the Christian Evidence Society.

to set forth the underlying unities of physical and religious knowledge ; the common foundations on which they really rest ; the similarities of methods, objects, and general results, which exist between them, and the actual identity of interests which binds them together, and which should be acknowledged in word, thought, and action.

CHAPTER I.

NO NECESSARY ANTAGONISM BETWEEN SCIENCE AND RELIGION.

Is there any necessary antagonism between Science and Religion?

This is the first and main question in determining their relations. This is the question which all well-wishers of either ought carefully to examine. For myself, I find the most thorough search showing an entire absence of any essential incompatibility. An apparent and *de facto* conflict exists, and has existed for centuries. But there is no required and rightful opposition. For if we look straight at them, endeavoring to distinguish them from the many other things that have borne their names and claimed their dignities, what are they? What, in strictness, is science? What, exactly, is religion? There are no authoritative definitions of either. There is, probably, no unanimous agreement in either the scientific world or the religious world as to the signification of either term. Many and various definitions have been proposed. There are few that are not imperfect. After a careful consideration, I think I may say, however, that the following ought to be accepted, as at least dealing fairly with both sides in the present question:

For science, there are, in the present day, two chief significations, differing, however, only in extent. In its broader sense it signifies *all systematized and trustworthy knowledge.* It takes, as its field, all that can be known with reasonable certainty, and affiliated with previous knowledge into a consistent whole. In its narrower and more special sense, science, in modern times, has come to be restricted to *that portion of systematized and certain knowledge which can be gained by a study of the physical universe.*

Religion has also two main significations:

1. In its most general significance it is *the expression of man's spiritual nature awakening to spiritual things.* As the spiritual nature manifests itself in the various channels of the human organism, this expression takes on various forms. Manifested through the intellect, it gives us religious knowledge or belief; through the heart, religious sentiments and attractions; through the executive organs, religious worship and action. This expression of the spiritual nature varies, of course, in strength, clearness, and elevation. In some, especially in savage races and early times, it is gross and feeble; in others it is intense, pure, and lofty. Primitively, it gave very likely only a sense of occult intelligent energies, animating the man, the cloud, the

wind, the sky, looked upon with fear, placated, shunned, or defied; ultimately, it rises to a recognition of a moral and spiritual being in man capable of eternal existence, and attains also a sense of an Infinite and Creative Spirit, on whom man is dependent, and to whom he owes gratitude, obedience, and reverence.

This is the broader signification of religion.

2. In a more special sense it is restricted to the particular beliefs or knowledges attained to in this unfolding of the spiritual nature. As these beliefs or knowledges form the justification for the sentiments and action which constitute the rest of religion, the first come to be spoken of as the whole of religion. Of these beliefs, some are inessential, some essential. Where the line should be drawn has been hotly disputed, and every one, almost, makes a different enumeration. It seems to me that only three can be properly regarded as necessary to the very existence of religion:

1. Belief in a soul within man.
2. Belief in a sovereign Over-soul without.
3. Belief in actual or possible relations between them.

Now, if the significations of science and religion may be taken to be substantially such as they have just been given, there is certainly no rightful antagonism between them.

Looking at the relations of the two from the

point of view of the first definition of science, i. e., systematized knowledge in general, then religion in its first signification, as the expression of man's spiritual nature, would be just a part of the facts which science is to study and systematize. The sentiments of gratitude and aspiration, the peculiarities of worship, the forms of belief which religious history exhibits, are just as much phenomena of the world, just as much facts of the Kosmos, as the markings of a flower or the transformation of a butterfly. Nay, they are the noblest and the most significant of phenomena, and Science could never claim to be complete if it did not receive them as a subject of inquiry and systematization. The result of such an inquiry and systematization of spiritual facts would constitute religious science. Religion, in the more special sense, "the particular knowledges or beliefs attained to by the awakening of man's spiritual nature," more or less coincides with this, and forms a subdivision of science, just in the degree that its doctrines are valid and systematically coördinated with each other and the facts which were their data. Normally, then, science is not complete till religion, in its general signification, becomes one of its objects of investigation, and, in its special signification, becomes a part of science itself. Science can no more have grounds for a quarrel with religion than she can have grounds for a quarrel with the phenomena of atomic affinity, molecular vibration and molar attraction and repulsion, or be at odds with the systematization of these phenomena into laws of chemistry and electricity, and with the inferring from them of chemical and electrical forces as causes. If the phenomena of religion appear incongruous with other phenomena, they are not therefore to be denied, or ignored, or ridiculed, but studied with the more care, as likely to reveal new laws and causes. If the laws and causes at present assigned to them seem erroneously inferred, it is the business of Science to assist Religion in making a better systematization of her facts.

Looking at the question next from the stand-point of the more special sense of science, the systematized knowledge derived from the study of the physical universe, then religion, both in its general and special sense, would, to a certain extent, stand outside of science. Science and religion would each have in a certain sense separate fields, or rather separate beginnings and points of view. They would not then be antagonistic, but supplementary. If, now, looking at different realms of the Kosmos, they should both come to the same result on any point, such as the existence of God or the soul, the agreement of such independent investigations would have especial weight. But, if they should fail to see exactly the same thing, this would not put them into antagonism, but rather would be what we should expect. Diverse posts of observation naturally give diverse views, especially when the subject of study, as in this case, is immense and complex. Positive testimony, of course, would have to be received from both, and united as well as might .be. But negative testimony from one side would be of no avail to contradict the positive testimony from the other. Because the touch feels none of the sound-vibrations of the air, this throws no discredit on the testimony of the ear that it hears sounds. The fact that the eye sees no odor come from the flower establishes no antagonism between it and the olfactory organ that smells it. If physical science reports that, neither by the balance, the dissecting-knife, nor the lens, it has found trace of any spiritual Being, this no more disproves the direct testimony of the religious faculties, that by their methods and organs they *do* find it, than the inability of the spiritual faculties to discover the laws of motion and matter disproves the testimony of science to them. If the investigation of Nature should not disclose anywhere (though I believe it does everywhere) evidence of a First Cause, this would no more contradict religion than the failure of religion to disclose the secondary causes of phenomena contradicts science. The word of each is good for its own account, and in its own sphere. Contradiction, and necessary antagonism, would arise only by one establishing the non-existence of the other's domain, and the entire fictitiousness of the sources of knowledge it claims, a thing which either of the two would have to step squarely outside of its own proper field even to begin to attempt. Modern physical science, especially, could not rightfully essay this, for one of its cardinal principles is the unity of the whole universe, the latent truth and reality of all persistent forces. In point of fact, the extreme outcome of modern scientific researches essays no disproof of the religious theories of the world, nor any demonstration that there is no God in the world, nor soul in man, but simply presents a confession of the insufficiency of physical inquiry to attain, as yet, by inductive methods, a similar result. Nay, it does not seek to deny, but it openly avows, that there is an infinite mystery behind and beneath all the phenomena which it studies, all the laws it has formulated, all the secondary causes it has reached. Some men of science, it is true, from this inability of their own processes, as yet, to fathom the mystery, deny that any method or faculty can fathom it. But this is no correct inference. It is, instead, a groundless, a thoroughly unscientific assumption. It is the faith of science that progress in knowledge is unending. The man of science must be always seeking. To identify the limit where progress is at present arrested with the absolute limit of possible knowledge is opposed to the whole spirit of modern inquiry. Nor, if Science concludes that its own methods and instruments are unavailing to reach religious truth, is that a reason for rejecting also the testimony which the spiritual faculties have from of old given to spiritual things? Rather, it is an admonition to the earnest seeker to turn in preference to this other oracle as the proper interpreter of the divine mysteries, and the better guide to its treasures.

From the scientific stand-point, then, there is no rightful quarrel between Science and Religion.

Is there any from the religious stand-point? What is there in this expression of man's spiritual nature, in any of its legitimate manifestations, that demands of it to draw a sword against knowledge of any kind? Which one of these expressions of the spiritual nature is it that needs to fight physical science? Is it love, aspiration, reverence, self-sacrifice, or any other of the religious sentiments? Is it philanthropy, purity, justice, consecration, or any other element of the religious life? Surely, none of these may properly combat science. Nor has the intellectual expression of the spiritual nature, the fundamental beliefs which, in a special sense, are called religion, any better reason for opposition to science. For the religious believer, just in proportion to the strength of his belief in the Creative Power, the Divine Omnipotence and Omnipresence, must believe that Nature is no independent power, man's perceptive and reasoning faculties no unmeaning or deceptive instruments, but that both physical and human nature are works of God, existing as he wishes them to exist, reflecting his mind and purposes, and therefore trustworthy witnesses of him. No opening of men's eyes to the facts of the world, no disclosing of the actual methods and laws of the Creation, can do any thing else (so the truly

religious should believe) than reveal the more clearly the existence and character of their Maker.   It
may reveal him as acting in ways that we had not
supposed.   It may compel Theology to revise its
schemes.   But this revision Religion must look upon
as received from God's own hand, and simply bringing us nearer the divine reality and truth.   He who
confounds the march of intellect with the operations of the devil, evidently inclines to trace his
own origin to Satan rather than to believe the word
of Scripture, that man was made in the image of
God, and that God saw all the works that he had
made, and behold they were good.   To the intelligent Theist, the record which the geologist deciphers in the rocks is a revelation written by the
same divine finger as that other revelation which
the theologian reads in the Psalms of David or the
letters of Paul.   To the enlightened Christian there
is truth to be learned about God everywhere in the
material and moral universe; and no religious studies can be regarded as complete or satisfactory that
neglect or ignore that grand source of divine instruction which God's handiwork presents to us.

CHAPTER II.

CAUSES OF THE ACTUAL ANTAGONISM OF THE SCIEN-
TIFIC AND THE RELIGIOUS WORLD.

RELIGION and Science, then, have no good cause
for antagonism, but rather for amity and sympathy.
Why, then, should they have had so many apparent
conflicts; why should there be so much jealousy,
suspicion, and ill-feeling, between scientific and religious bodies?

There are many causes. But the main ones are
these three: First and chief, *ignorance*. Few of the
religious have understood religion. They have been
familiar, of course, with its practical applications;
the forms of worship; the moral and philanthropical
duties which it has demanded. They have studied
carefully Scripture texts, and writings of the fathers,
and the creeds of the councils; but about the fundamental principles of religion, its real grounds, limits, and proper domain, there has been a great lack
of knowledge.

Similarly, few scientific men have really comprehended science. Facts of chemistry, of astronomy, of geology, they have learned with wonderful

2

thoroughness; but the principles of scientific investigation, its capabilities and limits, they have known little of. Physicists speak familiarly of scientific method, but "they could not," says Prof. Jevons,[1] "readily describe what they mean by that expression. Profoundly engaged in the study of particular classes of natural phenomena, they are usually too much engrossed in the immense and ever-accumulating details of their special sciences, to generalize upon the methods of reasoning which they unconsciously employ." Prof. Jevons's words find a noticeable illustration in the fact that the only considerable treatises upon scientific method, or the principles of physical inquiry which have been written in the present century, Mill's "Logic of the Inductive Sciences," Whewell's "Philosophy of the Inductive Sciences" and "History of Scientific Ideas," and Jevons's own "Principles of Science," are all the works of metaphysicians rather than of physicists, of mental philosophers rather than natural philosophers. And if few, either of the religious or the scientific world, have really understood the principles and proper limits of their own studies, still fewer have understood the principles and proper sphere of the other. Prof. Trowbridge, in a recent number of THE POPULAR SCIENCE MONTHLY, called attention to the insufficient acquaintance of

---

[1] Preface to "The Principles of Science," by W. Stanley Jevons, Professor of Logic and Political Economy in Owens College, Manchester, England.

ministers of religion with science. He quoted the courses of study presented in our principal theological schools, and showed how very small a measure of attention was given to physical studies, and how absurdly some preachers deliver their ignorant *ipse dixits* upon scientific topics. Although theologians are continually declaring, that the most dangerous enemy of religion to-day is science, they seem to have gained no realizing sense of the fact, and what it demands of them. They still imagine that the battle of the Evidences is to be fought on the field of ecclesiastical history, scriptural exegesis, and metaphysical postulates. They still practise with dictionary and concordance, as if the age of crucible and spectroscope had not come in. The great need of our theologians to-day is, to recognize the mighty turn which modern thought has taken, the new base of operations which it demands, and the new weapons it requires. As Hugh Miller said years ago, " Before the churches can be prepared, competently, to deal with the infidelity of an age so largely engaged as the present in physical pursuits, they must greatly extend their walks into the field of physical science." A hasty reconnaissance now and then to gather information to justify an attack is not what is wanted, but a careful and impartial examination of the scientific domain, and its relations with the religious realm. Even " from men who admire the progress of science," says Prof. Trowbridge, " I often hear sermons " which " do incalculable damage, by

drawing wide and unwarrantable inferences and con-
clusious from scientific facts."

Equally inadequate is the acquaintance of men
of science with religion. If there are among the
clergy parsons so impervious to modern knowledge
that they still believe that the earth is flat and immovable, and that the fossils of the Silurian period
are the remains of creatures drowned in the Flood,
there are likewise those who claim to be men of
science who are so ill-informed and undeveloped in
spiritual things as to doubt the usefulness of devotion, look on Christianity as a work of fraud, and
religion and morality as mere products of fear and
custom. It does not need to be argued, I think,
that religion is not a thing to be understood at a
glance by every one who is not a born fool. Spiritual things need special, systematic, thorough study for
their clear comprehension just as much as physical
things; and the man of science who essays, because
he is skillful with acids and alkalies, or has made
notable discoveries about sound, or heat, or protozoa,
to pronounce judgment on the problems of prayer
and providence, or the knowability of God, such a
man is just as likely to talk nonsense as the minister
who denounces Darwinism without having read a
tithe of the scientific expositions and evidence of it.
Yet it is not an uncommon occurrence, of late, to
see men of science indulge in such intellectual esca-
pades. Dazzled by their marvelous achievements in
measuring the stellar spaces and recovering the his-

tory of extinct species, physical investigators have fancied that Bacon and the modern instrument-makers have supplied them with the keys of universal knowledge, and with unhesitating confidence have pronounced from their scientific platforms just what the world must believe about divine personality, goodness, spiritual existence, and such other profound problems as the great Christian thinkers have spent their lives in finding and expounding the best solutions of. It is not strange if the religious world should be considerably amazed, and somewhat indignant, at the crude structures which have resulted when these scientific Babel-builders, taking atom and molecule for their only architectural materials, have essayed to push up their materialistic towers into the very heaven.

Now, this ignorance of themselves and each other has, and must, as long as it lasts, work evil to both religion and science. Unacquainted with the strength of each other's positions, they are prone to treat each other with indifference or contempt. Knowing not their own proper domain, or that of the other, they will be likely to encroach upon territory that is not their own, or consider themselves invaded or insulted without cause. The sight of blunders and bungles committed in these foreign excursions, tends to destroy their authority and respect for their knowledge in their own home-province. "Nothing leads thinking young men of scientific tendencies," says Prof. Trowbridge, "to neglect church-going more than wrong-headed and illogical deductions from science by their pastors." And, similarly, I may add, "nothing leads Christians to dislike and ignore scientific teaching more than the gross misrepresentations of pure religion too often given by scientific lecturers." It is those who are most ignorant of modern investigations, and most unfitted by their whole education to discern their bearing, who most freely launch the theological thunder-bolts at them, as impious and godless. And it is those who know least of the essence of religion and the grounds on which it is based, who sneer at them as old wives' fables, unworthy the serious consideration of any *savant*. Every such uncalled-for attack on one side or the other widens the breach between them. Could each know the other more thoroughly, most of this, I believe, might be escaped. As one of our American preachers said recently in an address to medical students,[1] "If the clergy could ramble with Mr. Huxley over the glaciers, and Mr. Huxley would take an excursion into the fields of Christian history, we should have better clerical sermons and better *lay sermons*."

Ignorance of themselves and each other is, then, the first and main cause of that antagonism between science and religion which, though it can have no *de jure* reign, has yet had an undeniable *de facto*

---

[1] Delivered to the graduating class of the New York College of Physicians and Surgeons, 1875, by Rev. E. A. Washburn, D. D.

existence. From this main cause there have flowed two subordinate ones:

1. A confounding of both religion and science with other things.

2. The claiming by each of exclusive knowledge, and, in consequence of it, a supremacy over the other.

These must be examined somewhat in detail.

First, ignorance of the true nature of religion and science has led to confounding them with other things. All science, certainly, does not deserve the sneering appellation which some clergymen are fond of employing—of " science falsely so called." But not a few things that pass for science have no real claim to the title. They are but metaphysical fallacies, probable hypotheses, or conjectures spawned in the fertile fancy of scientific dabblers, embraced by anti-religious prejudice, and wind-blown by conceit and love of sensation into every puddle of superficial Nature-knowledge.[1]

So it is also with religion. It is not all falsehood and masquerade; nevertheless, there is much, popularly set down as religion, which is no more religion than it is science. Now it has been bound up with one system, now with another. When

---

[1] " There is a great deal of what I cannot but regard as fallacious and misleading philosophy (' oppositions of science falsely so called ') abroad in the world at the present day."—(Dr. Carpenter's Address at Brighton, in 1872, as President of the British Association for the Advancement of Science.)

Christianity first raised its head, it was told that polytheism alone was religion. When Protestantism first ventured to send Christians directly and personally to the Bible and their own private judgment, religion, it was declared, meant simply the Roman Church, and all else was infidelity. In Augustine's day, Christianity was made inseparable from the doctrines of predestination and fatalism. In Abélard's time it was bound up with the metaphysics of realism; in Roger Bacon's, with the philosophy of Aristotle; in the days of Vesalius, with the medical treatises of Galen; in the lifetime of Galileo, with the astronomy of Ptolemy. To-day it is the orthodoxy of the Council of Trent or the Westminster Catechism that is cemented to religion, and any attack on the one is assumed to be undermining the very foundations of faith and morals.

Now, it is this false science, and this false religion—this confounding of other things, different in character, with these two great factors of human welfare (a confusion the more readily occurring because of the sanction that both the scientific and the religious worlds have given to it), that has led to the belief that there is a natural antagonism between physical inquiry and spiritual faith. These other powers may be natural opponents to Science, or natural opponents to Religion, or natural opponents to each other, and, walking in the guise of Science and Religion, readily give the appearance of a continual and rightful conflict between them.

There are metaphysical doctrines, for example, that are inimical to the very existence of religion ; and these metaphysical doctrines may happen to be adopted by certain scientific authorities, become current in scientific circles, and be expounded as if they were scientific truths. Auguste Comte, for instance, laid it down as the characteristic of the advance of knowledge from the Theological and Metaphysical stage to the Positive or truly Scientific stage, that it should be recognized that only phenomena, their coexistences and sequences, were knowable ; and Causes, especially the First Cause, beyond the possibility of our knowledge. Herbert Spencer, Prof. Tyndall, Prof. Huxley, and many other popular scientific authorities have, again and again, in scientific lectures and treatises, taken occasion to lay it down as one of the fixed things which the physical inquirer should recognize and respect, that the Supreme Reality is utterly unknowable. Were these, indeed, truths of science, then Religion would have no enemy more to be dreaded ; for, if the God whom she has worshiped and prayed to, and taken as her lawgiver, and believed that she has held communion with, is absolutely unknowable—then, indeed, no place is left for her on the earth. Not "worship, mainly of the silent sort," as Prof. Huxley advises, but the absolute suppression of every worshiping instinct and reverent thought, becomes

her. But, without discussing at all here this great
question of the knowability of God, I would point
out what hardly ought to be required to be mentioned, that this contest lies in a field quite outside
of the beat of Science. Science can declare what it
has found and *does* know, and what it has not yet
found out and does not yet know; but, as to what
it is *possible* or *impossible* to know, as to what are
the *necessary and absolute limits of the human mind*
—this is a question of *metaphysics,* not of science.
The whole argument proceeds through a discussion,
not of physical things, but of mental and spiritual—
laws of thought, analyses of consciousness, contradictions of logic. It is a question in which all the
chief arguments, *pro* and *con,* were elaborated before
modern Science was born. If scientific authorities
chose to borrow or reiterate what Lao-Tse, Kant,
Hamilton, or Mansel, have argued, that does not
transform the old metaphysics into modern science,
but simply exhibits modern scientists as amateur
metaphysicians.

Again, there are speculations and theories opposed to religion, which are often indulged in by
scientific men, and passed off for genuine science.
Such, for example, is the bald materialism that
would make matter the sum and substance of all
things; self-existent and alone immortal; life, its
complex product; thought, a motion of it; will,
the direction of its current. Such is the scientific
naturalism, still more prevalent, perhaps, among

physical inquirers, in which the uniformity perceived within the narrow field of human observation is set up as an absolute necessity ; succession of
phenomena is made the only reality ; its chain of
antecedents the only origin ; and its law the only
God. These theories may have a *quasi*-scientific basis ; they may be advocated by students, teachers,
and writers of the scientific world ; but, nevertheless,
they have no claim to call themselves science ; they
have never been accepted by a majority of the scientific world ; no proper and sufficient scientific authority, data, or reasoning, indorses them ; no scientific
verification of them is possible. Their dogmas, as-
suming for matter eternal and exclusive existence ;
asserting for our narrow experience universality and
necessity ; claiming, in regard to phenomena, a
knowledge that there is nothing more behind it
than is seen on its surface; denying altogether finite
or infinite spirit; repudiating the intuitions of
cause and substance—transcend altogether the experimental conditions which these same schools
make the limit of knowledge and the criterion of
truth. Inductive Science would have to renounce
its functions, and assume quite a different *rôle*, before it could legitimately make any such declarations. As Dr. Carpenter said at Brighton, in 1872,
in his address to the British Association for the Advancement of Science, " Those who set up their own
conceptions of the orderly sequence which they discern in the phenomena of Nature as fixed and deter-

mined laws, by which those phenomena not only
are (within all human experience), but always *have
been*, and always *must be*, invariably governed, are
really guilty of the intellectual arrogance which
they condemn in the systems of the ancients, and
place themselves in diametrical antagonism to those
real philosophers by whose comprehensive grasp
and penetrating insight that order has been so far
disclosed." And again, toward the close of his address: " When Science, passing beyond its own limits, assumes to take the place of Theology, and sets
up its own conception of the order of Nature as a
sufficient account of its *cause*, it is invading a province of thought to which it has no claim, and not
unreasonably provokes the hostility of those who
ought to be its best friends."

Or, to pass to the things that, in the name of religion, have opposed science : ecclesiastical hierarchies have always been, and almost inevitably are,
hostile to its progress. They are opposed to all progress. Their one great thought is, to preserve their
privileges, to maintain and heighten their authority.
When a religious movement grows into a church, it
is as when the young polyp grows into the coral.
At first tiny, soft-bodied, changeable, ranging at
will, as it increases in size it loses its freedom and
pliancy, attaches itself to some rock, becomes immovable, solid, itself a part of the rock. To new
ideas it can henceforth give, at best, only a stolid
apathy, a stony rebuff. Fortunate is the issue if it

does not heave its ponderous weight upon the rash dis-
turber of its peace, and crush him to powder. Alas!
how many tragic instances of this are written in blood
and fire upon the pages of church history! Colum-
bus, overwhelmed by the theologians at Salamanca
with biblical proof against a new world; Kopernik,
suppressing his heliocentric theory of the heavens
for thirty-six years, and escaping persecution only
by death; Galileo, tortured and compelled to recant
his declaration that the earth moves; Giordano Bru-
no, burnt alive for daring to assert a plurality of
worlds—such are the disgraceful illustrations of the
enmity of the Roman hierarchy to the progress of
physical knowledge. But do any of these facts show
a conflict between *Religion* and Science? Not one
of them. Neither the Roman Church nor any other
church is identical with religion. No ecclesiastical
body is synonymous with religion. All such bodies
are structures of men, social institutions. Religion
is no human construction, any more than the force
of gravitation, or the vital force, or the yearnings
of the loving heart. It is a force anterior to all
churches and hierarchies, the grand spiritual stream
flowing from above through the souls of men, of
which ecclesiastical organizations are but the earthly banks, the clayey reservoirs and wooden dams
by which men have thought they could better util-
ize the heavenly forces. Doubtless religion is in
the Church, and the Church more or less representa-
tive of religion; but by no means so exclusively and

purely is the Church filled and moved by religion, that the voice of the latter may be taken as the voice of the former. Besides religion, the Church has always contained, and still contains, much else—tradition, prejudice, love of power, superstition. The clamor of these often confuses and drowns the still, small voice of religion.

Again, theological dogmas and science have been, and still are, opposed. Theologians have formulated their dim guesses about God's character and ways into creeds, and imagined them finalities. They have speculated upon matters of purely physical knowledge, such as the antiquity of the earth and the age of man, the condition of the primitive globe and its inhabitants, the manner and method of their appearings, and have made these speculations into dogmas held as essential to religion. Thus, holding sway beforehand, by right of what might be called squatter sovereignty, over a large part of the field of scientific inquiry, and having consecrated as sacred edifices the rude and hasty structures raised by its early conjectures, when Science advances to take possession of its own, there results naturally a conflict. The different stand-points from which Science observes, the more thorough examination which it is its aim to make, give a more or less different representation of truth. Science must clear the ground of what it deems erroneous mental constructions before it can erect the systems which it believes **to be truer. And Theology has become so convinced** of the divine accuracy of its own models of the Creator and the creation, that if the old lines be altered ever so little, if new elements be suggested as constituting the constructive material, or an architectural power, different from that which the ancient guide-books narrate, be hinted at as the method by which it was built, or if even one of the withered ivies that had darkened its windows be pulled away, then it seems to Theology as if desecration had been committed, the creation robbed of its divineness, and the Creator banished into nonentity.

All theologies are liable thus to get in the way of Science; but in current Christian theology there are two dogmas in particular that have especially created antagonism. The first is the assumed infallible inspiration of the whole Bible; the second the assumed intervention of God in the order of Nature, or the special presence of Deity in that which is mysterious, exceptional, or lawless. In consequence of the first of these dogmas, there has been a struggle by theologians to limit modern science to the contracted circle of the ancient Hebrew knowledge of the universe, and any variation of statement from the letter of Moses or Job, David or Paul, is regarded as a dangerous loosening of another screw in the bonds of righteousness and the evidences of immortality.

In consequence of the second dogma, theologians have been jealous of any attempt at a natural explanation of the mysteries of the world, and have looked upon every extension of the realm of unbroken order and second causes as an invasion by Science of the religious kingdom. They imagine that one must lose whatever the other gains; that, step by step, as the arcana of the Kosmos are penetrated, and the same laws and substances are found ruling and constituting these, as rule and constitute the more familiar parts and operations of Nature, the action and presence of Deity must be denied, and the human mind landed more and more in the slough of a godless materialism.

But these also are antagonisms which faith is not responsible for, and which Theism does not command. These are quarrels in which pure and undefiled Religion is never present as a combatant. Theology is not religion, but the theoretical system men erect over and about religion. " The aspiring song of the spirit is one thing, the attempt to write its score, define its nature and explain its methods and its significance, quite another thing." There are many theologies, and each theology has many dogmas. Religion is an essence which was before all, which gave to all their original life, but remains identical with none. Least of all is it to be identified with a dogma that divorces ordinary Nature from God, confines his working to the dark corners of his creation, and recognizes him only where some overthrowal or interruption of his previous or customary work is supposed to be discovered. It is not only an equally religious view, but a far more religious view, it seems to me, that sees God present in every ordinary occurrence and lowest substance, pouring his will through the channels of unvaried law, and binding antecedent to consequent in an unflawed succession.

Neither is religion based on nor bound up with any one book. Had Abraham, Isaac, and Jacob, no religion, because Moses had not yet written? Was there no Christianity in the lifetime of Jesus, or the first forty years of the apostolic generation, before Matthew put his pen on to parchment? As well say that chemical affinity is based on Lavoisier's or Dalton's treatises, or that gravitation is ruined if Newton's "Principia" is shown false in a single theorem. Religion is the root from which what is divine and spiritual in Old and New Testament has blossomed. But the manifold other growths, of history, poetry, allegory, chronology, cosmogony, which pious reverence bound up in the same venerated chaplet, must not be confounded with the grand moral and religious truths that have given the ancient Semitic writings an incomparable place in sacred literature. "Physical and metaphysical science," to quote the Dean of Canterbury again,[1] "alike lie remote from the object-matter of revelation. Because God has in the Bible given us revelation in an informal way, in order, perhaps, to com-

---

[1] "Science and Revelation," by R. Payne Smith, D. D., Dean of Canterbury, Late Regius Professor of Divinity, Oxford. "Modern Skepticism," "Lectures of the Christian Evidence Society," p. 173.

mend it to our entire nature, people often forget
that its proper object-matter is simply the moral relation in which man stands to God, especially with
relation to a future state of being. Religious men
forget this. They often take up an antagonistic
position to science, and try to make out systems of
geology, and astronomy, and anthropology, from the
Bible, and from these judge all that scientific men
say. Really, the Bible never gives us any scientific
knowledge in a scientific way. If it did, it would
be leaving its own proper domain."

In fine, to come to the secret of the dissension,
new kinds of knowledge, or unusual theories of any
kind, naturally find themselves opposed by the old
beliefs—whatever be their nature—which occupied
the ground before them. The old is unwilling to
give up its time-honored reign. The new wants to
push out the old, to obtain more room for itself.
Now, what is old, whether it be really ancient philosophy, ancient custom,' ancient myth, or ancient

---

[1] Euripides, for example, puts the following into the mouth of
Greek orthodoxy: "The divine might is slow to come forth, but sure
nevertheless; and it chastises those mortals who foster insensate ob-
stinacy, who from mad opinion refuse to exalt the institutions of the
gods. Subtly and perseveringly do they hide their feet in ambush
and catch the impious man. For never should we indulge convictions and meditations which are wiser than established practices.
For cheap is the effort to believe that the Divinity, whatever else he
may be, is not powerful; and what comes from long time is established eternally, and inheres in Nature."—(Euripides, *Bacch.*, 882–
896.) The impiety here rebuked consisted in disapproving of Bac-
chanalian orgies!

physical speculation, or any thing else no more iden-
cal with religion, has always been apt to lay claim
to a sacred character. And what is new, whether it
be, in fact, new metaphysics, new religion, or new
speculation of any kind, is in these days equally apt
to dub itself by the title of Science. But surely the
old, merely as old, is no more to be identified with
religion than the new. Though tradition may always claim Religion as her champion, Religion is not
therefore responsible for Tradition's acts. Scientific
men, as well as priests and churches, have sought to
bolster themselves by appeals to the *odium theologi-
cum.* Even the illustrious Leibnitz charged the system of Newton with having an irreligious tendency.
And Religion, when new, is as apt as Science to be
accused of impiety. If any body of men were ever
filled with the thought of God, surely the early
Christians were; and yet, one of the charges which
the Roman polytheists brought against them was
that of atheism. It is not religion, then, but tradition, that opposes the new; and it is not the new
any more than the old that is the scientific. If all
uncommon theories and recent-born speculations be
science, how many scientific carcasses line the path
of history !

CHAPTER III.

THE CLAIM OF RELIGION TO POSSESS EXCLUSIVE KNOWL-
EDGE AND CONSEQUENT DIVINE SUPREMACY.—HU-
MAN CONDITIONS OF RELIGION.—DIVINE ORIGIN OF
SCIENCE.—HELP RECEIVED BY RELIGION FROM SCI-
ENCE.

SECONDLY, there are the claims made by both
Science and Religion of exclusive knowledge, and, as
a result of this, a rightful supremacy over the other.

I take up first the claim of Religion. It is one
of the most ancient claims of Religion that to her
has been given truth in its absolute purity, direct
from Heaven. Scientific investigations are but blind
human gropings. There is nothing divine or heaven-
descended in them. But religion is a revelation
from the Creator himself, conveying absolute and
final truth. No human admixture alloys its certainty; no sense-experience nor logical demonstrations are needed to make it credible; no further
principles are to be sought for. God has unveiled
to man in advance all the information about spiritual
things which it is essential for him to have. For
the human understanding to pick and dig about

these foundations is either superfluous or injurious.
If its investigations agree with the divine revelation, they are but a waste of energy. If they dis-
agree, they are beyond doubt mischievous mislead-
ings. Religious truths are not like scientific truths.
Spiritual phenomena are not like material phenomena. They are to be gazed at reverently, not searched
into with microscope and dissected with lancet.
They should be accepted in faith, not criticised by
impious reason. Of eternal and infinite importance,
as they are, what is man that he should set himself
up as their judge? "In the things of God," Mr.
Mansel tells us to-day, as Augustine, and Aquinas,
and Calvin, and Edwards, and the great Church authorities in every century, have told the world, " Reason is beyond her depth, and we must accept what
is established, or we must believe nothing."

Almost every branch of the Church claims more
or less of this exclusive knowledge. Each has some
oracle whose voice must be accepted as authoritative,
and whose message as divine truth, unmixed with
the dross of common human knowledge, needing
not that examination and verification which other
kinds of truth require before it is worthy to claim
man's credence.

At its lowest term, this oracle is merely the
spiritual intuition, the voice within the breast. In
its next higher form, it is the word of the religious
master; in Islam, of Mohammed; in Buddhism, of
Sakya-Mouni; in Christianity, of Jesus. At a third

stage, it presents as infallible every verse of some sacred book—Veda, Koran, Bible. At its highest term, the Church, or, perhaps, its official head, High-priest, Grand-Llama, Mikado, or Pope, becomes the vicegerent of God, and the exclusive declarer of divine truth.

Believing that in herself she has thus a special, direct, and unerring source of divine knowledge, Religion naturally is disinclined to admit the possibility that she has made mistakes, or that Science is competent to correct her, or to find out religious truths undiscovered by her. The investigations of Science are very well as long as they confirm the Scriptures, and sustain the Church ; but to stray from the ortho-dox pathway, to criticise or contradict what Penta-teuch or Papal College has laid down, is a sacrilege. Evangelical Protestantism, by instance after instance, has disclosed its unwillingness to allow to Science any other position than that of a subordinate and a satellite ; and the Roman Church has explicitly and officially declared the absolute supremeness of the Church in all such matters, and the wickedness of looking upon Science as capable of correcting the interpretations of the Church. In the General Coun-cil of the Roman Church, held in 1870, known as the Vatican Council, it was defined to be "a doc-trine divinely revealed, that when the Roman Pontiff speaks *ex cathedra* . . . . he possesses that in-fallibility with which the Divine Redeemer willed his Church to be endowed. . . . The pastors and

faithful, of whatever rite and dignity, are bound by
the duty of hierarchical subordination and true obedience " in reference to doctrines thus defined by
the pope. And in regard to human science, in particular, the position previously taken by the Papal
See was ratified by the formal decree:

" Let him be anathema—

" Who shall say that human sciences ought to
be pursued in such a spirit of freedom that one
may be allowed to hold as true their assertions even
when opposed to revealed doctrines;

" Who shall say that it may at any time come to
pass in the progress of science that the doctrines set
forth by the Church must be set forth in another
sense than that in which the Church has ever received and yet receives them."

Language such as this makes it plain that, whatever be the tendency in the more liberal Protestant
communions, the Roman Church has no thought of
abandoning the theories of human and cosmic origin
which it has planted itself on in times past, or en-
couraging any study which would naturally or probably lead to doubt of the authority of the Church
which has enunciated them.

Ancient and common as is this claim of Religion,
I believe it to be erroneous. It cannot stand before
thorough criticism and sound logic. Religion has
no exclusive source of information, but such sources
only as are common to all branches of human knowledge. Every oracle that has ever been set up in the

Church, as the voice of the Divine, has had and still has its human conditions and vehicles. I would not deny the great fact of revelation, proceeding from God, for the enlightenment of man. We come to perceive religious truth—yes, and secular truth also, I rejoice to believe—not merely by our own unaided efforts, but by the help of the divine illumination constantly vouchsafed to the earnest seeker after truth.

But, living in the world in which we do, within the material organisms in which our spiritual natures are embodied, possessed of no other knowing faculties than these finite ones of ours, how is it possible for us to receive divine truth in its absolute fullness and purity? How can man either apprehend it, or interpret it, or know it as divine, without the revelation becoming subject to those finite limitations which are the conditions of human thought?

However undoubtedly and exclusively a revelation may have had its beginning with God, how can it reach man's consciousness except through the sensitive and rational avenues of the organism in which God has set man's soul? And these perceptive avenues will inevitably give shape to the message that passes through them. These mental windows will tint with the color of their own glass whatever light streams through them.

The pint pot cannot hold a quart. The earthy soul cannot take in the spiritual conception. Love, aspiration, self-sacrifice, divine communion—these

are but sounds without sense to the carnal mind.
Though Jehovah speak in clearest tones the law of
righteousness from Sinai's summit over the Hebrew
host, what is it to the flocks and herds? what is it
to the mixed multitude whose mouths are watering
for the flesh-pots of Egypt? Only so much thick
cloud round about, and the sound of thunder and
the blare of a great trumpet. Only to Aaron and
Moses comes intelligible meaning. Verbal commu-
nications, holding however lofty spiritual truth, are
but jangling noises to a man unless some corresponding idea exists already in the man's mind which may
welcome the message and make plain its signification. They will either be rejected as meaningless,
or drawn down from their noble height to some
lower level on which they can be grasped.

It has been said that, if a Polynesian cannibal
was told that he ought to love his enemies, he would
answer, " Yes, we do—both roasted and broiled ! "
There are authentic anecdotes showing equally de-
graded transformations of religious conceptions when
introduced to savage minds. When Burton spoke
to the Eastern negroes about the Deity, they eagerly
asked where he was to be found, that they might kill
him, for, they said, " who but he lays waste our
homes, and kills our wives and cattle ? "

" Why did you baptize that Iroquois ? " asked a
Huron Christian of a missionary. " If he gets to
heaven before us Hurons, he will scalp us and turn
us out."

3

The sun sends forth his radiant beams as pure white light. The full luminous stream bathes impartially the whole earth. It comes to rock, to flower, to element, absolutely the same. But with each it becomes something quite different; for each untwists the woven ray, and selects from it a diverse hue, according to its own inward affinities. The atmosphere picks out its blue; the leaves draw to themselves the emerald; the iris chooses the purple; the buttercup paints itself with the yellow; the cardinal-flower sucks its cells full of the scarlet. So it is with the illumination that the soul receives from the Sun of Righteousness. There is one and the same light, but what is received from it varies according to the capacity of the recipient. As the largeness of soul in the man, and the generousness with which the soul's doors are opened, vary, so do the measure of inspiration and the character of the revelation. Each man's God takes its figure and dimensions from the ideal of his own sense of justice, or truth, or love. It is the image of himself projected on the screen of the Infinite. To savage tribes, Deity is but a mightier warrior; to over-burdened, enervated races, the unspeakable peace of a Nirvana; to the oppressed and down-trodden, he is the righteous avenger and judge; to the tender and loving, he discloses himself as the pitying, ever-caring Father.

In coming even to the first earthly recipient, then, revelation must take on human phases and

become subject to finite limits. And if from the
first recipient it is carried abroad over the world,
and down through generations, it must subject itself
still more to human conditions and uncertainties.
Traveling from man to man, it subjects itself to the
errors attendant on verbal or written communication. Proceeding from nation to nation, it becomes
liable to the distortions attendant on translation from
the tongue of one into that of the other. Passing
from a personal, inward feeling or thought into
the external symbols or speech that may communi-
cate to others the truth felt within, it is exposed to
the imperfections of language and to the errors of
interpretation. There is no system of speech or
written signs that can more than very inadequately
represent the delicate shadings of our mental con
ceptions. There is no arrangement of material
symbols, whether of letters or of sounds, that can
more than very coarsely image the subtile qualities
and delicate character of spiritual things. While
the Divine thought, which is the source of revelation, is, of course, infallible, yet how can it find any
infallible form of words in which to clothe itself?
And if in the past this has happened, yet, when
the usages of language change from generation to
generation so greatly and rapidly as they do, where
shall we find an infallible interpreter to tell us their
exact meaning to-day? Or, if one be found, who
shall infallibly interpret for us his explanations?
We must fall back on our own fallible understand-

ings at last, for the sense of whatever revelation or interpretation is given to us.

Again, how are we to know that what comes to us claiming to be a revelation is really one? Here, again, the only judge is the fallible human conclusion of our own reason. "It must be plain," as has well been said, "that as far as revelation contains any truth that asks mental assent, it must appeal to the mental faculty. No one denies this, unless he masks clear sense under some mental sophism." The lofty claim made when a divine revelation is asserted does not thereby free the claim from the possibility of dishonesty or error, but makes it all the more important to determine whether the claim be a true one, or the pretended revelation be only some mistake, or delusion, or trick of priest or lying spirit. Were there but a single claim made of such a kind, still, faith would not be exempt from the duty of examination and verification. But when, as is the case, numerous conflicting claims are made; when Buddhism, Mohammedanism, Christianity, each brings forward that divine revelation, it becomes an absolute necessity for faith to discriminate what it deems the false revelations from what it deems the true revelation. And, in doing this, it must take guidance from its natural presuppositions, its own sense of the right and the true, its own experience of the good.

A man may suspend his reason in obedience to the authority of a church. But, in order to come to

take such a step, he must first employ that reason to
bring him to a belief in the duty of so doing, and to
select the church that rightly, in his opinion, possesses
such a claim. John Henry Newman, it is said, declares that "the true Catholic is not he who believes in the Church because it is right, but he who
submits implicitly to it without presuming to ask
such a question." Nevertheless, how can even the
Romanist have intelligently come to the decision
that he ought to surrender his reason to the Church,
unless by persuading himself that history and experience show the claim to be a reasonable one?

Either Faith adopts its authority unreasonably,
unintelligently, by the mere accident of birth, or
circumstance, or caprice, or else she must have some
reason for her choice; must have sought, that is,
the arbitership of human understanding, and found
that approving of the claim preferred. A revelation
which would not allow of such a confirmation, by
the prepossessions of our reason, no thinking man
can accept as divine. Even the man to whom immediately the knowledge of a divine truth is im-
parted could have no faith in it without such a rati-
fication of it by his own sense of truth.

Suppose, for example, that to-day a spirit descended from heaven and revealed personally to us
that the Ruler and Creator of the universe is a man
of flesh and blood and stature, as ourselves, or a
six-armed, eagle-headed being, such as Hindoo idols
represent him; or suppose this messenger from the

other world should bring us, as a message from God, some farrago of nonsense, some plain contradiction of our moral and religious principles, what intelligent man would put the slightest faith in it? Who would not say that either it was an hallucination of our sense, a deceit of some trickster, or if, indeed, a spirit-messenger, then, a messenger from the pit, not from the heavens.

Do you say the truth of the revelation is shown by miracles? Passing by the primary objection that no outward sign can overweigh the inward sense of truth, how can a miracle convince a man except by appealing to his judgment and experience? What else is it but an argument from the analogy of human life, that every effect has a cause proportionate to it; that these phenomena are above that order of things with which man is familiar, or which he can cause; and, therefore, as supernatural effects, must have a supernatural cause? And on what else does the cogency of this argument depend than upon a previous conviction of the veracity of God; a conviction derived partly from the human intuition of the same truth, partly from man's experience of Divine goodness and faithfulness. Unless we believed beforehand both in God's existence and in his honesty and kindness, no message, no matter how miraculously authenticated, would be of such significance as either to invite our belief or even be worthy of much attention.

Such human conditions and necessary imperfec-

tions, in general, beset religious as all other knowledge. And, in particular, we may ask, where can
faith show us any infallible oracle free from possibility of mistake and human limitation ? Will the
Church furnish us with such a superior source of
knowledge ? The Church is but a congregation of
fallible men, and cannot eliminate from its sum total
what is contained in every individual part. History
shows but too conclusively how far from infallible
both Church and pope have been. In its unflatter-
ing mirror, the oracle of Rome is exhibited as con-
victed of error in scientific matters, again and again ;
compelled to retreat from position to position ;
forced to correct and recorrect its interpretations.
It is shown vacillating to and fro in regard to the
most important ecclesiastical questions ; possessed
of no clear or well-defined principles concerning
many essential theological issues ; the successive
popes refuting and overturning each other's decisions ; its councils annulling the bulls of the popes,
and branding them as heretical, and its popes fulmi-
nating anathemas against its councils.[1]

If this be the course that consists with infallibility, its advantage over fallible sources of knowledge is undiscoverable.

Or will the Bible furnish us with an infallible
authority ?

Study its pages with a careful eye, and see. Does

[1] *See* "The Pope and the Council," by Janus. Translated from
the German. Boston : Roberts Brothers. Pp. 42–62.

it claim anywhere to be absolutely, throughout its whole extent from Genesis to Revelation, free from error? Nowhere.

What Paul says refers only to the Old Testament, for no gospels, and but few epistles, were then written; and what he asserts is that all Scripture is God-inspired—that is, filled with the breath of God—not infallible. And the particular purposes for which it is profitable he specifies. It is not for scientific knowledge, but " for teaching, for reproof, for correction, for discipline in righteousness, that the man of God may be perfect, thoroughly furnished unto every good work "[1] (2 Timothy, iii. 16, 17).

The claim of Paul, criticism must admit. The Scripture *is filled with the breath of God*, and profitable for moral and spiritual culture. In it undoubtedly " men of God spake as they were moved by the Holy Spirit." But to the eye that would find in the Bible a flawless record, exempt from human liabilities, a different answer is given. Variations of style and diversities of thought meet it. Discrepancies of fact and inconsistencies in statement, which all the wearisome toil and subtilties of commentators have failed to reconcile, confront the inquirer. What is prescribed by the law is swept away by the prophet. What is said by them of old time is repealed by the Christ. Paul shows the worthlessness

[1] Translation of Geo. R. Noyes, D. D., late Hancock Professor of Hebrew and other Oriental Languages at Harvard University.

of works, and James the nothingness of faith without them. The evangelists quote mistranslations from the inaccurate version of the Septuagint with more frequency than from the supposed infallible Hebrew. The narratives of Genesis fail to agree with the records God has written in rock and bone-cavern, in fossil, language, and star. The list of books considered inspired was gradually formed, and has differed at different periods. Books now called apocryphal were formerly a part of the canonical Scriptures. Books formerly rejected as apocryphal are now reckoned as a part of the divine record. It is not improbable that in the course of time portions of the present canon may be transferred to the Apocrypha.

The text of the Scriptures is by no means free from doubt, nor even from confessed error. As it now stands in our received version, the existence of no small number of erroneous readings and acknowledged interpolations is a fact known to all scholars. For an accurate test, there is no single manuscript that we can resort to. We must rely upon the critical judgment of certain fallible men to select, out of many codexes, the particular word which in each passage they judge the most likely to be the original. Surely this is not the spectacle that should be presented by an authority "without mixture of error."

Surrendering, then, the Church and the Bible, may we find in the Christ an authority exceptional and absolute ?   I desire not to deny the existence of a divine element in Jesus. I gladly recognize him as the loftiest spiritual seer and teacher the world has seen ; the best historic embodiment of spiritual perfection that we have. But we must own, if we are clear-sighted and frank, that in Christ himself we do not yet obtain an oracle exempt from the limitations of humanity and the conditions of earthly knowledge. There was in him the human as well as the divine. "The Word was made flesh and dwelt a mongus;" and through that fleshly brain and tongue it saw and spoke what it saw, using the language of the day, addressing itself to the conceptions and issues of the age. Acute critics have shown clearly in the life and teachings of Jesus the influence of the epoch and nation that environed him. They have pointed out in the Jewish literature, preceding and contemporaneous to his career, the elements of his instruction and parallels to many of his most striking sayings. In regard to those ideas of his which were opposed to the prevalent ones of his times, it should be remembered that a reaction against current ideas is not uncommon, and as much a natural result of them and evidence of their influence, as conformity to them. That wonderful and incomparable flower, whose beauty shines forth from Galilee over the whole world, did not, nevertheless, grow suspended in the air without contact with any thing else, but was sprung from a Jewish root, elaborated by Jewish nutriment, and tinted with Jewish hues. Only so could Jesus have got into such close contact with his age and nation as to gain the leverage whereby to fulfill his providential mission of giving to it a motion and a revolution that should in time extend to all quarters of the globe.

Or, lastly, may we find in the conscience of man, in his intuitions of truth and duty, or in his instincts of worship, an infallible oracle? This voice within the heart is a channel through which the Universal Spirit most immediately breathes its inspiring influence. To each individual it is his personal oracle, his final authority. But, to furnish us with an unerring source of moral or religious knowledge, with an absolute authority, it has no claim. For whose intuition, what man's conscience, what nation's moral sense or religious instinct, shall we take as our standard? That of the Indian Thug, or that of the Buddhist who thinks it a sin to kill a flea? That of the Feejee parricide, or that of the filial Christian? That of the worshiper of idols, or that of him who worships God as a Spirit in spirit and in truth? Every student of history knows that the voice within the heart varies its answers in every degree of latitude and longitude; has as many differences of expression and detail as the individuals in whom it whispers.

Thus, whatever authority Religion may choose, none of them can give her absolute truth, none can exempt her from the limitations and conditions of human knowledge. The attempt of humanity, by

any standard-building it can perform, by any selection and exaltation of one expression of itself over
another, to free itself from its native fallibility, is
as futile as the mediæval search for a universal solvent. If any one says he possesses the universal
solvent, pray, in what sort of a vessel does he keep
it? If any one says he has an infallible oracle,
pray, by what faculty did he find it, by what
power does he now know it, comprehend it, and
transmit to others its decisions without loss of that
infallibility? A man's natural fallibility, as has
well been said, obviously cleaves to him like his
own personality, and infects every decision which
he makes.

And, as Religion must recognize that her knowledge is not free from the human conditions and
characteristics which belong to Science, may not Science not unlawfully claim for its knowledge also par-
ticipation in that same divine origin which Religion
has boasted of as its sole prerogative? Is not science, on one side at least, from God—a missive tell-
ing of the Divine existence and character? If we
ask the Christ, we find him from field-lily and wild-
sparrow drawing instruction as to the love and care
of the heavenly Father. If we ask of Paul, we receive as answer, " The invisible things of him from
the creation of the world are clearly seen, being understood by the things which are made, even his
eternal power and Godhead." If we ask of the
Psalmist, the response comes again: " The heavens

declare the glory of God, and the firmament showeth his handiwork; day unto day uttereth speech,
and night unto night showeth knowledge." Or, if
we look for ourselves, what do we find? These
fauna and flora which Science describes are not its
inventions. The hieroglyphics in the rocks which
it deciphers are not of its construction. Science
finds them there because they are there; and they
are there, every monotheist must say, by the permission, by the creation of God; for, unless we go back
to dualism or polytheism, we must recognize God
as the sole author of all things. Whatever facts or
laws exist in the world are there because such was
God's will; whatever relations of God to Nature,
whatever aspects of the Divine government, are disclosed by physical investigations, are disclosed because God himself first drew the picture, and then
gave to man the eye with which to see it. As we
discern, in the manner a house is built, the character
of its builder, what sense of beauty he possesses,
what carelessness or faithfulness, what folly or wisdom, characterizes him, so, in the peculiarities of the
kosmic temple, we may discover the attributes of the
Great Architect. Whatever God has done, whatever
God is doing, is an expression of his nature. Every
fact, then, which Science can tell the world, every
law it can unravel, every force it can trace out, has
some divine message for man. Every natural phenomenon, be it bacteria in sealed flasks, or colored
bands in a spectrum, be it building power of mole-

cule, mimicry of insects, natural selection among animals (provided only it be actual fact, not guess of
man), has something to tell us of God's thoughts,
and powers, and methods of action.   All science is
thus a revelation of the Omnipresent Worker; every
new discovery a fresh epistle from the creative Spirit to all the churches of knowledge.   And is it reverent to look on this grand unveiling of Nature's
mysteries, these sublime disclosures of infinity, eternity, unity, and order, which Science has given us,
as things coming without any of that inspiration
from above which we credit to the advent of religious knowledge?   Was it so much easier a thing to
discover the laws of planetary motion than to discern the moral principles laid down in the ten com
mandments?   Is it so much less noble a thing to
write the history of God's universe than the history
of the tribe of Judah?   That seems to us the most
worthy view of inspiration which limits it not to
scribes, nor prophets, nor apostles, but makes it
the light of all our seeing, the impulse of every
noble effort, the uplifting force in every spiritual
ascent.   It guides the studies of a Cuvier as well
as the legislation of a Moses; it animates the
thoughts of an Agassiz no less than the songs of a
David.

   Religion, then, I say, cannot rightfully claim to
be the sole source of knowledge.   She possesses no
lawful sovereignty over the realm of Science, but
stands on the same ground of experience, employs

the same human faculties, is subject to the same fallible conditions, as Science, and in her divine message receives not an exclusive privilege, but one given likewise to her comrade. How unwise, then, is it for her to seek to discredit Science, to endeavor to obstruct its progress, to reject the new light physical inquiries are affording, and angrily to denounce the new conceptions of Divine existence which they are introducing! Religion cannot aim a blow at Science without wounding herself. If Religion forbids us to trust God's own handwriting on the tablets of Nature, how can she expect the world to accept the revelations which have come to us in each case through the distorting medium of human faculties? If Religion forbids us to trust the original documents which are open to every one's inspection, how can she expect us to receive the record which has descended to us down a long line of transmissions, transcriptions, and translations, at the hands of fallible men? If Religion refuse to receive the corrections of Science, and repulse her proffered assistance, how can she escape the pitfalls of superstition, how can she rise to the intellectual heights, where she can see the divine truths with unobstructed vision?

For Faith, though she be the great heaven-climber, climbs with but half-open eye, in only a twilight light. The pure and exalted spiritual truths which Religion enjoys to-day were by no means the original immediate perception of an infallible faith-faculty, nor the primeval possession of a privileged recipient, but they have been attained only by the efforts of thousands of generations who have successively "felt after God if haply they might find him;" and thus groping, straining their intellectual eyes, have so refined and purged the inward sense that the ever-present reality has become clearly perceptible. Not by a single bound has Religion sprung to the mount of vision, but step by step she has patiently toiled upward. " The glimmering wonder of original fetichism; the wider feeling expressed in Nature-worship, of an omnipresent secret of power; the higher consciousness breaking forth in historical, prophetic religions, of the connection between this reverence for the Supreme Majesty and all loyalty of soul," not only has each of these been a phase through which Religion has had to pass, but the transition from one to the other has been by numberless gradations; and it has been because of the criticisms and discoveries of Science, more than any thing else, that this ascent has been made. It is only as the tides of wider knowledge have worn away terrace after terrace of the alluvium of superstition, that Religion has mounted to the loftier and immovable rocks of fundamental truths. It is only as physical inquiry, with iconoclastic hammer, has broken idol after idol, that Faith has transferred her embrace to the purer objects, worthy of worship. And as Religion is indebted to Science for this progress of the past, so for the future it is only by the same aid that she can expect further advancement. Instead of turning to Science the cold shoulder, Faith should not only welcome but invite her coöperation.

CHAPTER IV.

THE CLAIM OF SCIENCE TO POSSESS EXCLUSIVE KNOWL-
EDGE AND RIGHTFUL SUPREMACY.—THE FAITHS OF
SCIENCE.—ITS GROUNDS AND METHODS SIMILAR TO
THOSE OF RELIGION.

THE time, however, has gone by in which Science needs much help against Religion. At the present day the physicists can very well take care of themselves against the religious. The religious world, to a considerable extent, is learning to lower its pretensions. The old claims of the exclusive possession of an absolute knowledge and of a rightful supremacy in all matters of belief are fast dropping away. Science, by the most intelligent in the religious world, is coming to be recognized, not as a subordinate, but as an independent power; not as a hostile rebel, but as a friend•and fellow-laborer. But, unfortunately, as the one side is dropping its dogmatism, the other side seems to be picking it up and clothing itself with it. The infallibility now to be feared is not so much that of the pontiff, who fulminates his excommunications from the Vatican, as that of the scientific popes, who essay, from professors' chairs, to lay down the precise boundaries within which Belief may now walk. The oracle that now claims an exclusive insight and certainty, that looks upon other avenues to truth with contempt and disbelief; that would absorb, if it could, all other authority in its own, is not so much Religion as Science.

Look, for example, at the very word *science*. At the present day it is commonly employed in reference to *physical* knowledge. Such an expression as the "science of religion," or the "science of God," strikes us as unusual. It seems to involve a figurative extension of the word beyond its proper sphere. Yet, until a hundred or two hundred years ago, sci ence denoted merely knowledge in general, or, in a more special sense, systematized knowledge of any kind. Shakespeare speaks of "music, mathematics, and other sciences." In the middle ages, the science *par excellence*—which would have been supposed to be referred to, if the general word was used for some particular but unspecified branch of knowledge— was the science of theology. To express the science of Nature, it would have been necessary to join with it some qualifying adjunct.

The change in the use of the word indicates a great revolution in thought. It is an interesting historical witness to the wonderful achievements of physical investigation, and to the lofty claims that it makes at the present day. "I alone," modern Science tacitly says, by the very name by which it designates itself, "I alone am *scientia*, real knowledge; all else is more or less guess-work."

And this is not merely a tacit assumption, an unconscious arrogance, but a claim which men of science nowadays are very fond of publicly proclaiming. The certainty of science is contrasted with the uncertainty of other branches of pretended knowledge, especially with that of religion. Science, it is declared, is most careful in its requirements of proof before it gives credence, Religion most careless. Science carefully examines Nature and life to see what things really are, builds up its laws by an inductive accumulation of fact upon fact, and then demands that every generalization be experimentally verified before it is accepted as true. Religion, on the other hand, with pious credulity mounts any vaulting hypothesis that the Church may order her to ride, leaps heroically upon it, up mistformed *high-priori* roads, toward the highest heaven, and, as she whirls through the dizzy heights, lets down link after link of deduction with as much confidence as if the chain were fastened to some immovable support. Auguste Comte classes religion with metaphysics, as but "products of the world's crude infancy." "Science," says the great positive philosopher, "conducts God with honor to its frontiers, thanking him for his provisional services." Huxley presents against Religion the charge that "with her the belief in a proposition, because authority tells

you it is true, or because you wish to believe it,
which is a high crime and misdemeanor when the
subject-matter of reason is of one kind, becomes under the *alias* of faith the greatest of all virtues when
the subject-matter of reason is of another kind;"
and he would enforce upon us the wise advice, as he
calls it, of Hume: "If we take in hand any volume
of divinity or school metaphysic for instance, let us
ask, Does it contain any abstract reasoning concerning quantity or number? No. Does it contain any
experimental reasoning concerning matters of fact
and existence? No. Commit it, then, to the flames,
for it can contain nothing but sophistry and illusion."

Such are the charges currently made nowadays
against the trustworthiness of the truths of religion; such are the unfavorable comparisons made
against its methods and results as compared with
those of science. Not a few men of eminent repu-
tation in physical investigation have lent themselves
to it. More of lesser knowledge have loudly exulted
in it; and many and many who have got some little
smattering of modern science have thought to show
their superior enlightenment by most extreme charges
against the validity of religious knowledge.

Now, I would freely admit that there has been
and still is, among what has been currently accepted
as religious truth, a great deal that has not been so
certain as it should be. Theology has advanced ex-
aggerated claims to absolute knowledge. It has indulged in most groundless hypotheses. It has made

most unwarranted assumptions about the plans and counsels and inmost nature of the Godhead, and about the details of the future life, and about scores of other things entirely beyond human power to know. Creeds have laid down dogmas about human nature and Scriptural inspiration, the authority of prophets and apostles, the work and deeds and nature of Christ, that have shown themselves plainly contradictory to observation and experience, to reason and the moral sense.

Mediæval scholasticism especially sinned grievously in these respects. It delighted in hair-splitting disputations over frivolous puzzles and in endless speculations about things not only transcending the possibility of human knowledge, but destitute of any practical moment. Its only criterion of truth was the deliverances of the Church or the almost equally venerated Aristotle. When Bacon turned the human mind to the pursuit of the useful and the study of natural things, and enjoined the method of induction and the test of verification, knowledge made amazing conquests. The human atom, looking forth from his petty pellet of planetary matter, has measured and weighed the celestial bodies, traced their orbits through the heavens, divined the processes by which they grew from dusty nebulæ into glowing sun or life-blessed planet; he has tracked the subtile Proteus, Force, from form to form, and made it now fly with his messages and then drag him on his errands, and spin, and knit, and reap, and sew for him.

It is not strange, therefore, that physical science should have grown somewhat conceited, and imagined that its pet methods and its own narrow circle of work were alone compatible with any solid attainment.

And the religious world for the most part has unwittingly confirmed this assumption. Finding the researches of modern science in geology, astronomy, ethnology, and so on, bringing up formidable objections to current religious doctrines, instead of saying, "Religion knows only the truth: if the received doctrines are shown to be inconsistent with any fact, let them be revised"—instead of thus honestly acknowledging the possibility of some past errors, and removing from religion the burden of sustaining portions found to be erroneous or doubtful, the religious world, for the most part, has clung to the most incredible parts as if they were its most essential elements; and it has sought to justify them by declaring that the unconverted reason is incapable of comprehending the high mysteries of religion. Religious truth (theologians and preachers, defending the old beliefs, have maintained) belongs to another realm from ordinary kinds of truth. It is not to be tried by the understanding. It is not to be brought to the bar of common-sense—but it is to be discerned by the inner soul, and its evidence found in the soul's satisfaction in it. By this view, which has been advocated and defended by such men as Hamilton, Mansel, Baden Powell, and Faraday,

the field of truth is divided into two separate portions: one, the province of knowledge, where science holds sway ; the other, the province of belief,
where Religion has her throne. The two, however
opposite they appear, can never, it is declared, really
interfere or trouble each other. Science may establish that, scientifically, the sloth, and the humming-
bird, and the kangaroo, and a thousand other species
of living creatures, could not have come from Australia, and South America, and Greenland, across
seas and icy deserts, to take shelter in Noah's ark.
Scientifically, then, it is not to be credited—that is
all. But, as a matter of religion, it is none the less
to be accepted. It only requires more of that faith
without sight by which the believer should walk.

Now, by taking this mode of defending itself
against the incursions of modern science, the Church
has aided much in spreading suspicion of the certainty of its cherished doctrines. When its own
advocates would make a believer's mind like those
vessels that are built with water-tight compartments,
one-half of it for the play of common-sense, the
other for the dwelling-place of faith, such troublesome things as reason and observation being securely
locked out when the soul is at its devotions, or considering its creed—it is exceedingly likely that those
practically inclined should judge this realm of faith
to be not a realm of fact, but of fancy. Bishops like
he of London may exhort the modern inquirer as
eloquently as they please to throw away doubt as

they would a bomb-shell: but it serves only to make the investigator more suspicious of the validity of religion. He beholds science challenging for itself full and searching scrutiny, but his spiritual guides hiding away religious truth as much as possible from his inspection. He sees science becoming more firmly established the more vigorously it is criticised. He beholds Theology, meantime, grudgingly and ungraciously, but continuously, yielding up, before the steady advance of scientific investigation, one after another long-cherished dogma. The entire circle of religious truth falls under doubt. That which is declared to be beyond the depth of reason he suspects is only a turbid shallow of superstition; and this faith, which is not knowledge, will never do for practical men who seek realities. The only thing which seems to the modern inquirer entirely worthy of confidence is science, and to that he looks, in mingled fear and hope, to see what loved belief it shall next sweep away, or what modicum of religion, if any, it shall discover at last a scientific justification for.

Now, if it be the fact that knowledge is only to be found within the special circle and by the special methods of physical science, if religion has nothing equally certain to show, then, it seems to me, the fate of religion, among all educated men, is already sealed; and the wise will seek as soon as possible, in museums and scientific institutions, the only Teacher who can declare abiding, trustworthy truth.

4

And, moreover, as long as there prevails the current, unrefuted *suspicion* that it is so—as long as the religious world sanctions expressly or implicitly the idea that theology requires, to use Huxley's phrase, "a different measure and a different weight from science," it will be impossible for it to disarm the hostility of scientific minds, it will be impossible for it to maintain its foothold in society against the steady *crowding out* which physical discoveries are constantly exercising upon it. If the religious domain in the modern mind is not to become such a domain as Strauss charges that it already is, "a domain resembling that of the red Indians in America, reduced to constantly narrower limits by their white neighbors,"· it must be shown that, in its essential elements, it possesses certainty, not *absolute* certainty—for we are learning that for man there is little or no absolute certainty—but the same kind and measure of certainty as men act upon in trade and daily life, and especially accept unhesitatingly in science.

In the last century Bishop Butler wrote a famous argument in which he showed the analogy of religion to the course of Nature, and that the same sort of difficulties that are found in it are found also in the constitution of Nature. It presented strongly the inconsistency of those who, accepting Nature as the work of a wise and good God, halt before the difficulties which they descry in the course of revelation. But that argument, well put as it was, has lost its effectiveness against the doubters of religion to-day. For its corner-stone, the doubter's belief in Divine Creation, is just the thing now called in question; and the exhibition of difficulties in Divine Creation similar to those in revelation, instead of leading the inquirer to accept both, rather inclines him to throw them both overboard. The method of that argument, however, has always seemed to us a good one, *provided* only some corner-stone which the doubter thoroughly accepted as solid could be found from which to start the *reductio ad absurdum.*

Now this corner-stone seems to be furnished at the present day by physical science. It is, as we have just noticed, the oracle of almost every religious doubter, the arsenal from which he draws most of the arrows he casts against religion, the rival for the suffrages of belief with which religion is unfavorably contrasted—the substitute, in fine, which his instincts of reverence and worship put in the place of God and constitute his Divinity. Now, if it can be shown that the same difficulties attend this unquestioned science as attend religion, and that religion, whether or not it has absolute proof, yet has just as good proof as that which in physical matters all accept, the doubter, it seems to me, will have little ground left to stand upon, and the practical trustworthiness of religion will be shown.

Now this, I believe, can be shown. Knowledge is not a special privilege of natural science. The proofs and evidences of religion are just as valid.

For most of them are strikingly similar, not a few identical. The grounds, and methods, and results of spiritual knowledge are, in the main, either the same or closely analogous to those of accepted physical truths. The common charges made against religion are applicable also against contemporary science. Science cannot discredit religion without invalidating its own work; and those who unhesitatingly accept all the deliverances of physical investigation ought logically to accord the same belief to the similar proofs which Religion presents of her main theses.

This similarity between religious and physical knowledge is what I aim to set forth in the next few chapters. The subject divides itself into two great divisions : I. A comparison of the grounds and methods of science with those of religion ; II. A comparison of the objects aimed at and the results reached by the two.

I. The grounds and methods of science compared with those of religion.

The means of gaining knowledge are various. There is—

1. Personal observation and experience furnished by the senses. This may be either (*a*) original ; or (*b*) in verification of something already discovered, testified to, expected, or predicted.

2. Intuition. This comprehends (*a*) immediate cognition of consciousness or direct mental perceptions, and (*b*), corresponding to these, constitutional convictions universal and necessary among the bulk

of mankind—convictions suggested and developed by experience, but before personal experience existing as native predispositions, moulding and making possible experience, and, when developed, extending their affirmations beyond the limits of all experience.

3. Testimony. This may be either (*a*) in witness of a fact, that is, evidence, or (*b*) in the shape of an opinion or judgment of some one presumed to know; that is, authority.

4. Inference, by which these various data are worked up. This may be either (*a*) deductive, that is, reasoning from the general to the particular; or (*b*) inductive, reasoning from one quality in many to the same in all; or (*c*) analogical, reasoning from similar qualities in one to the accompanying qualities in the same.

Again, inference may be either (*d*) demonstrative, reaching certitude; or (*e*) probable, approximating more or less to certitude, reaching at one end of the scale moral certainty, at the other amounting simply to a theory or hypothesis.

Now, it is a prevalent notion, especially among those who unfavorably contrast the methods of religion with those of science, that of these various methods, science uses almost entirely the following four: sense-observation, induction, deduction of experimental tests, and verification; and has little or nothing to do with the opposite methods: intuitive cognition and belief, evidence, authority, analogy, and other kinds of merely probable inference. Religion, on the contrary, it is charged, neglects almost entirely the first set of methods, and trusts herself unwarrantably to the last.

Huxley, for example, in his lecture upon the "Educational Value of the Study of Natural History,"[1] states what he says is the method of all science, and it consists of simply the four steps just mentioned. Newton declared that hypotheses are not to be regarded in experimental philosophy, but only observations and inductions. Prof. Tait says: "Natural philosophy is an experimental science. No *a priori* reasoning can conduct us demonstratively to a single physical truth." Comte will not allow introspection as a source of valid knowledge. "Positive philosophy," according to him, "knows only sense-observation and the various inductions and deductions that may be made from it." Hippolyte Taine says, in reference to the general ideas which correspond to real qualities, that "they are the object of the experimental sciences, and their connections are discovered by the *inductive* road."[2] Lewes similarly condemns intuition as having "no such safeguard" as sense has. "The method of verification, let us never forget," he says, "is the one grand characteristic distinguishing science from philosophy, modern inquiry from ancient inquiry. . . . The proof is with us the great object of solicitude. We demand certainty; and as the course of human evo-

[1] "Lay Sermons," p. 83.
[2] "On Intelligence," p. 409.

lution shows certainty to be attainable on no other method than the one followed by science, the con- demnation of metaphysics is inevitable."¹ And Prof. Tyndall, in his answer, in the *Contemporary Review*, to the critics of his prayer-gauge sugges- tion, after acknowledging that the theory of an over-ruling God who answers prayer is a legitimate theory, says, " but, without *verification*, a theoretic conception is a mere figment of the intellect."

Now, no such division or contrast in the meth- ods of science and religion exists, I believe. If they be taken up successively, it will be seen, I think, that science, on the one hand, employs intuitive cog- nition and belief, authority and evidence, analogies, hypotheses, and various probable inferences, as well as religion; and, on the other hand, that religion, like science, grounds itself on observation, induction, and experimental verification. In short, science has its faith-basis, and faith its scientific foundation.

I. Let us consider first the faith-basis of science. Take, to begin with, intuition. Here has always been one of the chief bulwarks of religion. It is from the immediate cognition of consciousness that religion affirms that it derives those spiritual phe- nomena, personality, free-will, devotional sensibility, and aspiration, and those great ideas, right and wrong, duty, responsibility, infinity, perfection, divinity,

---

¹ "Biographical History of Philosophy," pp. xxix., xxx., Intro- duction. In his "Problems of Life and Mind," *passim*, the same thing is said again and again.

which constitute its foundations. And it is to the native convictions, universal in humanity, of a great Superhuman Spirit, and of a longer life for the human soul than its life in the flesh—convictions at first perhaps dim and vague, possibly mere predispositions to this view rather than that, but with experience and intellectual development becoming clearer and more elevated—that religion refers as among the strongest proofs of its truth.

Men of science, however, as we have already noticed, have entertained the greatest hostility to and scorn of intuition; and have made it one of their chief objections to theology that it trusts so confidingly to it. Nevertheless, intuitive cognition and conviction is the only ground upon which science can rest a large part of its own fundamental doctrines. Science, for example, accepts as the most trustworthy of all its departments the science of geometry. The truths established by it are indispensable to astronomy and to much of mechanics and physics. Yet, how is the truth of the fundamental axioms of geometry known? By sense-observation? No skill and care would ever enable us to learn or prove experimentally any one geometrical proposition in the absolute way in which we know them all. Any finite amount of difference vastly less than what the sense could discern would falsify them. Yet the most delicately measured and constructed figures are but rude approximations. They may seem equal where they are unequal, and regular where they are irregular. In fact, there are in Nature no unextended points, no breadthless lines, no even planes, no exact circles and spheres, such as geometry deals with. Our diagrams might *suggest* such truths as that the sum of the angles of a triangle are equal to two right angles, and that the square on the hypothenuse is equal to the sum of the squares on the other two sides. But they never could make it absolutely certain. Our exact and absolute knowledge of these truths is known, just as the axioms of morality are, by the mind's eye, by the direct inner apprehension.

Or in any of the physical sciences, take up any so-called simple fact of observation, and see how, instead of the observer and his fact standing in direct relation, there is a perfect chain of successive intuitions between them.

A botanist, for example, relates to a scientific society that he saw last week the phenomenon of a perfectly green rose. But how, Mr. Botanist, do you know that you really observed such a thing? You saw it, you say, with your own eyes. But how do you know your eyes are to be trusted? Perhaps you say that you smelt it or felt it, also. Still, let all the senses testify to it, how do you know they do not all deceive you? It is possible. The best observer may make mistakes.[1] Every sense is liable

---

[1] Astronomers have long recognized, under "allowance for personal equation," a certain inexactness in the observations of the best observers.

to erroneous suggestion.[1] Every morning we wake from a crowd of fallacious perceptions, and our open-eyed moments are but waking dreams. Taine calls perception, in his work on "Intelligence," "essentially hallucination," so liable does he show it to be to deception, and so constantly does it refer sensations to localities of the body where they do not really exist.[2]

[1] Either an excitement of the nervous centre by hasheesh, opium, alcohol, or some intense idea, or an irritation of the nerve by concussion or local inflammation, is sufficient, as repeated experiments and observations have shown, to excite illusions of the senses. Such volumes as Maury's "Annales Médico-Psychologiques," Baillarger's "Des Hallucinations," Griesinger's "Traité des Malades Mentales," Abercrombie's "Inquiries concerning the Intellectual Powers," or any standard "Pathology" or "Physiology" will illustrate this point.

[2] Taine, in Part II., Book I., Chapter I. of his "On Intelligence," shows by numerous instances cited from medical authorities, that while we assign every sensation which we experience to a certain place in our sensory members, foot, hand, tongue, etc., this is but an illusion. When a foot has been amputated, tinglings will be felt for many years, as if in the foot no longer there. Disease in the marrow excites tinglings in the extremities. When a new nose is formed by turning down a flap of skin from the forehead, and the nose is touched, it still seems for a long time to be the forehead that is touched. The sensation, though usually excited by some external object, may be excited by some molecular disturbance in the nerve, or by an image in the cerebral lobe. The affirmative judgment, or mental perception, none the less follows. We call it then a case of hallucination. But as in all cases the presence of this internal sensation is the immediate antecedent—as it is this internal phantom which is taken for an external object—all perceptions are really hallucinations. "Thus external perception," he says, "is an internal dream. . . . The hallucination which seems a monstrosity is the very fabric of our mental life."

"Of course," says the botanist, "I am liable to mistake a false perception for a true one, but whatever is really perceived is infallible evidence for its own truth." But what is "really perceived?" When the actual observation is rigorously analyzed we find that what is actually observed is not any external thing, but certain inward states of consciousness which we call sensations—sensations of color, smell, touch, etc. As Mill,[1] and Bain, and Taine, have shown in the field of philosophy, and Huxley, and Spencer, and Helmholtz, have reaffirmed as representatives of science, all that we really know of any

[1] John Stuart Mill, in his "Examination of Sir William Hamilton," Chapter XI., defines matter as a "permanent possibility of sensation," and will not believe in matter in any other sense. "I do not believe," he says, "that the real externality to us of any thing, except other minds, is capable of proof."

Prof. Helmholtz, in "The Recent Progress of the Theory of Vision," says: "What we directly apprehend is not the immediate action of the external exciting cause upon the ends of our nerves, but only the changed *condition* of the nervous fibres, which we call the state of excitation or functional activity."

Prof. Huxley, in his address on Descartes, "Lay Sermons," p. 340, says, emphatically: "Matter and force are, so far as we can know, mere names for certain forms of consciousness. . . . Thus it is an indisputable truth that, what we call the material world, is only known to us under the forms of the ideal world."

Herbert Spencer, "Principles of Psychology," p. 206, says, after an extended review of the relativity of feelings: "Thus we are brought to the conclusion that what we are conscious of as properties of matter, even down to its weight and resistance, are but subjective affections produced by objective agencies that are unknown and unknowable."

object is nothing more nor less than our knowledge of certain forms of our own consciousness. There is no observation, strictly speaking, of any external object. We must either say, with Prof. Bain and his school, that "the belief in the existence of any portion of matter outside and independent of our consciousness is a most anomalous fiction," or else we must rest for its truth on an intuitive conviction of the veracity of the senses and the existence of an external world such as would give rise within us to our felt states of consciousness.

Again, you say that you saw the rose last week. Still more intuitive beliefs must you, then, lean upon. For, how can you testify with certainty to what occurred last week? You have no present sensation such as you describe. You have only in your present consciousness an image or recollection of it, and how do you know that this present image is a truthful copy of the past sensation? There is no reason for it except that intuitive conviction of the veracity of memory which John Stuart Mill himself is forced to acknowledge as an "ultimate belief."[1] No past experience can prove this trustworthiness of memory. For it must in each case be taken for granted before you can have any cognizance whatever of your past experience.

But still another intuition belongs to the chain. You said that it was *you* who observed the rose last

[1] Mill's "Examination of Hamilton," p. 216, vol. i., American edition.

week. You remember it as an experience of yourself, and you imply, and the worth of your testimony depends upon the fact, that you who a week ago had a certain sensation, and now have it not, are yet one and the self-same person. Now, how do you know this personal identity? Again, you must admit you know it only by an intuitive conviction.

Thus, to be able to trust the simplest past observation of a natural object, we must accept these four intuitive beliefs: 1. In the veracity of the senses; 2. In the reality of an external world; 3. In the veracity of memory; 4. In our continuing personal identity.

Among the fundamental principles on which science depends are the three doctrines of the indestructibility of matter, the continuity of motion, and the persistence of force. Were it possible for matter to become non-existent, or for motion or force to lapse into nothing, there would exist in science incalculable elements, fatal to all positive knowledge or scientific interpretation of phenomena. What warrant have we, then, for the truth of these great principles? Inductive experiment? This has certainly contributed much to establish it. Delicate tests with balance and retort have shown that when matter, motion, or force, seemed to disappear, they simply changed their form, place, or direction. Solids changed to gases, molar motion to molecular motion, force of heat passed into magnetic or chemical force. Track the cunning Proteus into his new haunt, and you will find him there undiminished in quantity. This is what experience has suggested and approximately proved. But it has only done so approximately, never absolutely. It has shown that the more delicate were its means of measurement, the more closely it could follow every diverging motion or escaping matter, the more nearly equivalent was the quantity accounted for at the end with that with which the experiment began. But it has never proved this with any absolute exactness, nor for any larger field than the narrow circles which have been specially investigated.[1] Moreover, all through the so-called process of inductive proof, the truth to be demonstrated has been continually assumed, as Herbert Spencer has admirably shown in the fourth, fifth, and sixth chapters of his "First Principles." Whatever inductive experiments are made depend for their validity upon the continual assumption that the gravitation of the weights, or whatever unit of force is taken as the measure, remains constant, and of this, says Herbert Spencer (p. 187), no proof is assigned, nor can be assigned. "Nor is it only in their concrete data," he continues, "that the reasonings of terrestrial and celestial physics assume the persistence of force. They equally assume it in the

---

[1] Prof. Joseph Lovering, in his address as president, before the American Association at Hartford, 1874, says of the doctrine of the conservation of energy: "The most that physical science can assert is, that it possesses no evidence of the destructibility of matter or force." *See* also Lewes's "Problems of Life and Mind," vol. ii., p. 262.

abstract principle with which they set out, and which they repeat in justification of every step. The equality of action and reaction is taken for granted from beginning to end of the argument; and to assert that action and reaction are equal and opposite, is to assert that force is persistent. . . . Clearly, then, the persistence of force is an ultimate truth of which no inductive proof is possible."

Or take the other great basic principle of science—the uniformity of Nature, embracing in that term both the uniformities of coexistence, or accompanying qualities of things, and the uniformities of succession, or, as Mill calls it, the universality of causation. The validity of all induction, of all reasonings as to matter of fact in past, present, or future, depends upon the assumption of this uniformity of Nature. What scientific foundation, then, does science present for this universal basis of its knowledge? It has none. John Stuart Mill, to be sure, sought to rest this general basis of induction upon induction itself, even upon an induction by simple enumeration.[1] But all his logical skill could not cover up the fact that he was thus proving the universal by a limited number of particulars, the greater by the less, the stronger by the weaker. It hardly needs to be pointed out that any particular experience, short of universal extent, cannot prove

[1] "I hold it to be itself an instance of induction, and induction by no means of the most obvious kind."—(" Logic," Book III., Chapter III., § 1.)

a universal law. However the evidence be manipulated, a general and absolute conclusion cannot be established upon a limited and uncertain premise. Experience can only testify as to what has been, not as to what will be. It can testify to what has come within its field, not as to what is outside. Although two events have accompanied each other a hundred thousand times under our observation, that is no proof that they will do so the next time. It is possible that they may not. As one whose predispositions all lead the other way says, "Water has quenched our thirst in the past; by what assumption do we affirm that the same will happen in the future? Experience does not teach this; experience is only of what has actually been ; and, after never so many repetitions of a thing, there still remains the peril of venturing upon the untrodden land of future possibility. The fact, generally expressed as Nature's uniformity, is the guarantee, the ultimate major premise of all induction. 'What has been will be,' justifies the inference that water will assuage thirst in after-times. We can give no reason, no evidence, for this uniformity; and therefore the course seems to be to adopt this as the finishing postulate."—(Bain's "Logic," I., 273.)

This is, indeed, the only logical course, to admit the belief in the uniformity of Nature as a fundamental postulate, a primary intuition, an ultimate law of the mind. As Bain says in another work ("Emotions and Will," second edition, page 537),

" The foremost rank among the inductive tendencies involved in belief is to be assigned to the natural trust that we have in the continuance of the
present state of things." This natural trust is not,
as Mr. Mill would have us believe, a mere generalization from experience. Experience may confirm it,
but it exists before experience. It is what makes
experience possible in the first place, and afterward
shows it to be applicable.

But it may be said that, though there is something in this natural trust, this intuitive belief, that
precedes the experience of the individual, it does not
precede the experience of the race ; that it is, in fact,
simply the experience of our ancestors, organized
within us. This is what Herbert Spencer and Lewes
urge. But, should this be established or admitted, it
would give no sufficient explanation to our present
question. The question here is, not about the origin
of our belief, but about its logical validity. Grant
that the experience which testifies is not merely that
of the individual, but that of the whole human race
from its creation, or, if you please, that of the still
longer line of man's ancestry from the lowest living
creature up to the humanity of to-day, this is still
far from sufficient to afford logical validity to belief
in universal uniformity. After even this extension
back through all past generations is given to experience, the portion of time and space which it can bear
witness to is but a little corner in the great field of
Nature, and the induction of the premise still falls

immensely short of the universality which the conclusion demands. Unless Science acknowledges that
its fundamental principle has no logical justification,
it must rest it on the intuitive conviction or natural
faith of men in it, and recognize such natural faith
as an ultimate foundation, sufficient as its own evidence, allowing nothing lower and needing nothing
stronger beneath.[1]

2. Authority and evidence. Every religion leans
upon these more or less. Every religion has its
founder, prophet, or teacher, whose word it rev-
erences. Before the disciple sees the truth of his
master's teaching by his own mental sight or life-
experience, he accepts it as true; presuming that it
is true because he recognizes in his master a knowledge and a nature superior to his own. The precious
utterances of such masters are collected in books,
which soon become sacred. Some Holy Scripture,
Bible, Koran, or Veda, is an heirloom in every form
of faith. Then comes the need of evidence to prove

---

[1] The following passage from Huxley's address on Descartes's "Discourse," "Lay Sermons," p. 327, might be quoted in confirmation of
the points so far made: "Strictly speaking, the existence of a 'self'
and of a 'not-self' are hypotheses by which we account for the facts
of consciousness. They stand upon the same footing as the belief in
the general trustworthiness of memory and in the general constancy
of the order of Nature, as hypothetical assumptions which cannot be
proved or known with the highest degree of certainty which is given
by immediate consciousness." Although we should prefer the name
"intuitive beliefs" to "hypothetical assumptions," yet the argument for the *faith*-basis of science is the same.

the important questions of its authenticity and genuineness. The longer a form of faith endures, and
the farther away it gets from its original fountain,
the larger place in it do these two elements naturally take. In Christianity, especially, great stress has
been laid upon them. With many it has been an
undue stress, that neglected the internal evidence
that would still remain for Christianity though all
external evidence were swept away. Nevertheless,
there is a natural and proper place for authority and
evidence among the proofs of the Christian religion.

And in science, too, there is a similar need and
use of these two media of proof and personal conviction. All beginners in science, and the great
mass of common people, have to lean upon scientific authorities.[1] Some few scientific facts and laws
they can observe or form for themselves. But for
all the more difficult matter they must trust some
one or ones whom they believe to possess competent
knowledge. For example, even such a universally-
believed fact as the revolution of the earth around
the sun—there is not one man in ten thousand who
has mastered personally the proof of it, or who is
able to demonstrate it to any man who should de-

---

[1] "Authority is the evidence on which the mass of mankind believe every thing which they are said to know, except facts of which
their own senses have taken cognizance. It is the evidence on which
even the wisest receive all those truths of science or facts in history
or in life, of which they have not personally examined the proofs."—
(John Stuart Mill, "Three Essays on Religion," p. 78. *See* also
Le Conte, "Religion and Science," p. 236.)

clare himself a believer in the old Ptolemaic system. The other nine thousand nine hundred and ninety-nine accept it as a fact through their faith in a few astronomers' assertions.

Prof. Henfrey, in his paper upon the "Study of Botany,"[1] takes pains to deny that it is indispensable for every prosecutor of natural history to verify or repeat the propositions of the abstract science; "in fact," he says, "the enunciation and demonstration of them, which form the great business of the philosophical botanist, would scarcely come within the space of possibility for the generality of mankind busied with other matters." This is equally true of almost every other branch of science. If the student of physical knowledge should accept nothing on authority, he would spend his life in retracing a few hand-breadths of early investigation. Progress is made in science, as everywhere else, by accepting in faith the results of the past, and making them a platform on which to mount higher. Not only scientific pupils must do this, but all beneath the very great masters; and even these greatest masters must do so outside of their own specialties. Even among those who stand high in scientific fame, how many, for instance, who accept and use the results of Laplace's "Mécanique Céleste," Faraday's electrical discoveries, Champollion's and Bunsen's Egyptian discoveries, Rawlinson's and Oppert's decipherment of the cuneiform inscriptions,

[1] Youmans's "Culture demanded by Modern Life," p. 105.

or William Thomson's measurement of the size of molecules, have ever themselves followed through and verified the steps by which those results were reached?

Nor can science progress without a similar trust in and use of evidence. In chemistry, to be sure, most facts can be verified at any time by experiment. But even here it is not more than once or twice that a chemist will evaporate forty tons of mineral water, as Prof. Bunsen did, to show in it a little cæsium. Chemists, for the most part, are content to take Bunsen's testimony for it. In astronomy, the eternal stars generally allow instant verification of observation at any time. But for transient and exceptional facts, the testimony of a few, perhaps of a single observer, has to be relied upon. And it is relied upon, though the facts often are in apparent contradiction to the usual order of Nature. When Tycho Brahe relates that he one night saw a star flash forth in great brilliancy in the constellation of Cassiopeia; or Prof. Young describes immense eruptions upon the surface of the sun as witnessed by him; or some other observer at a remote point of the earth tells of an eclipse seen only there, science confidently accepts their evidence. So, for the dates of ancient eclipses and planetary conjunctions, the occurrence of meteoric showers and the appearances of comets in former times, astronomers rely upon ancient records whose authenticity and genuineness are, to say the least, no more sure than those of the first three gospels or the Pauline Epistles. This method of comparing present observations with former ones is a frequent one with astronomers, and their main resource in determining exactly the length of the day, the year, and other natural constants. Hipparchus made the first clear application of it, it is said, when he compared his own observations with those of Aristarchus, made one hundred and forty-five years previously. Laplace, in explaining the long inequality in the motions of Jupiter and Saturn, was much assisted by a conjunction of these planets observed by Ibyn Jounis, at Cairo, toward the close of the eleventh century. Poisson, by making use of an ancient eclipse recorded by the Chaldeans, was supposed to have proved that the sidereal day had not altered one ten-millionth part in twenty-five hundred years. Similar calculations were made by Laplace. It is now concluded, however, that the sidereal day is longer by one part in two million seven hundred thousand than in 720 B. C. All these calculations, of course, assume the trustworthiness of ancient records.

In geology, botany, zoölogy, also, the man who will believe nothing but what he has seen with his own eyes will learn very little. No one observer can personally observe a thousandth part of the phenomena which constitute the accepted stock of scientific knowledge. At most, he can but scan a *hortus siccus*, or museums of minerals, shells, skeletons, and stuffed specimens. For the original locality and position of strata, for the living appearance, habits, and homes of the various species, and for the whole account of the fauna and flora of remote countries not yet illustrated by accessible specimens, the man of science must depend upon the reports of travelers, often no more in number than, nor so close in agreement as, the Four Evangelists. They bring back reports of glass sponges, and animals with eyes brought up from the rayless and plantless depths of the sea, as in the recent dredging expeditions. They give us accounts of fossil horses, no bigger than a fox; of veritable dragons, the winged-fingered pterodactyles, twenty-five feet from tip to tip; of birds with well-developed teeth in both jaws, and of fish with legs; of sea-serpents, the sauroid reptiles of the Cretaceous period, over seventy feet in length—as Prof. Marsh's expeditions have done. They tell us of a race of dwarfs and other marvels, as Schweinfurth has done; they recount every day new wonder after wonder, just as much opposed to general experience as any thing in the doctrines and accounts of Christianity, and the scientific world receives their narratives with full credence. Certainly, scientific men should be the last to refuse as credible the testimony of honest eye-witnesses simply because their narratives contain some marvelous details.

3. Analogy, hypothesis, and various kinds of merely probable inference.

Religion, it is true, often uses these in support of the doctrines it advances. It employs the argument from analogy, for example, in proof of the future life of the soul. Every atom of matter, it says, is believed by Science to be absolutely indestructible. So also is every smallest quantity of force. If these other units, if all the rest of the force in the universe is thus able to survive the shocks of change, if all else is thus carefully guarded by Nature from destruction, is it likely that the intelligent soul, the conscious unit, the spiritual force which is the most exalted of all earthly things, perishes at the end of this short life?

Again, every order of organized sentient being below man has a sphere of development and action commensurate with its capacities. Unless man be a solitary exception to the general order, he must also have such a sphere. But it is evident that in this hand-breadth of earth and earthly life his vast capacities and desires cannot fulfill themselves. If his chances of development are like those of his fellow-creatures, he must have an existence hereafter to give the opportunities not supplied here.

Now, whether these analogies be considered as supplying logical proof or not, they are just such as Science uses.

Science asserts with entire confidence the existence of this and that chemical element in the heavenly bodies, iron and sodium in the atmosphere of the sun, Sirius, and other stars; blazing hydrogen gas in the dumb-bell nebula and other irresolvable nebulæ. How does it know any one of these facts, say the last? Simply by the fact that objects on the earth presenting the same spectroscopic lines are hydrogen. As the nebula presents these lines, it is inferred to be of the same constitution in other respects also. It is by a like analogical argument that the white spots at the poles of Mars are believed by scientific men to be snow, that the fossil skeletons found in the earth are held to have once belonged to living animals, and that the likenesses of composition and growth which language and geological strata exhibit, teach us their history and origin.[1]

[1] In Dr. W. B. Carpenter's "Inaugural Address before the British Association for the Advancement of Science," at Brighton, 1872, I have, since writing the above, found the following confirmatory passage: "Mr. Lockyer speaks as confidently of the sun's chromosphere, of incandescent hydrogen, and of the local outbursts which cause it to send forth projections tens of thousands of miles high, as if he had been able to capture a flask of this gas, and had generated water by causing it to unite with oxygen. Yet this confidence is entirely based on the assumption that a certain line which is seen in the spectrum of a hydrogen-flame, means hydrogen also when seen in the spectrum of the sun's chromosphere; and high as is the probability of that assumption, it cannot be regarded as a demonstrated certainty, since it is by no means inconceivable that the same line might be produced by some other substance at present unknown."

From Prof. Whitney we extract the following in regard to the use of analogy in philology: "So far back as we can trace the history of language, the forces which have been efficient in producing its changes and the general outline of their modes of operation, have been the same, and we are justified in concluding—we are even compelled to infer—that they have been the same from the outset. There is no way of investigating the first hidden steps of any continuous historical process, except by carefully studying the later recorded steps and cautiously applying the *analogies* thence deduced. So the

5

Of course, the knowledge derived in this way, whether by science or religion, is but inferential, and, moreover, merely probable. He must be very ignorant of Science who reproaches Religion with the employment of inference or merely probable arguments, as if she alone were a sinner, or guilty above her physical sister. Science is as much the daughter of reason as of the senses. If the first step in induction is observation, the second is always what inference the observations justify. It is from this point of view that Herbert Spencer gives as one definition of science, "an extension of the perceptions by means of reasoning" ("Recent Discussions," p. 160). Observed facts do not deserve the name of science until they have been arranged by the magnet of some idea and marshaled in the onward column of some argument. "Isolated facts and experiments," says Helmholtz, in his lecture upon the "Aim and Progress of Physical Science" ("Popular Lectures on Scientific Subjects," p. 369), "have in themselves no value, however great their number may be. They only become valuable in a

geologist studies the forces which are now altering by slow degrees the form and aspect of the earth's crust, wearing down the rocks here, depositing beds of sand and pebbles there, pouring out floods of lava over certain regions, raising or lowering the line of coast along certain seas; and he applies the result of his observations with confidence to the explanation of phenomena dating from a time to which men's imaginations, even, can hardly reach. The legitimacy of the analogical reasoning is not less undeniable in the one case than in the other."—(Whitney's "Language and the Study of Language," p. 253.)

theoretical or practical point of view, when they make us acquainted with the law of a series of uniformly-recurring phenomena; it may be, only give a negative result, showing an incompleteness in our knowledge of such a law, till then held to be perfect. . . . To find the law by which they are regulated is to understand phenomena."

Science, then, supplies no valuable knowledge till its crude facts are crystallized by inferences, and built up into conclusions. And it is rare, in physical investigations, that these conclusions are more than probable. There are some cases, of course, where our investigation may be made exhaustive. Such are the cases where our inquiry is limited to a small class, a definite portion of matter, a moderate extent of time or area of space. But in almost all cases, not alone in analogical reasoning, but in the best inductions, in all those which much advance knowledge, our conclusions must pass beyond the narrow confines of our data. "In natural history," says Prof. Henfrey,[1] "it is rarely in our power to ascertain all the particulars requisite for any given induction; it is scarcely ever possible to use this demonstrative induction. We are continually obliged to derive a general consequence from a portion of the particular cases which it ought to rest upon, and in such cases we anticipate the agreement of the rest, basing the hypothesis upon analogy. In this way

[1] "The Study of Botany," Youmans's "Culture demanded by Modern Life."

we arrive, not at absolute certainties, but at great probabilities." Similarly says Prof. Youmans, now the editor of *The Popular Science Monthly*, speaking of the study of biology,[1] "Complete or demonstrative induction being impossible, we are compelled to form conclusions from only a part of the facts involved, and to anticipate the agreement of the rest.". So, also, says Prof. De Morgan, speaking of induction : "Since it is practically impossible to examine all particulars, the statement of a universal from its particulars is only *probable*, unless it should happen that we can detect some law connecting the instances by which the result when obtained as to a certain number may be inferred as to the rest. . . . This induction by connection is common enough in mathematics, but can hardly occur in any other kind of knowledge."

Whenever we get a clear idea of the vast numbers of permutations and combinations which may be possible with no very great number of various agents or conditions, we learn how hopeless it would be to attempt to treat Nature in detail, and make exhaustive inductions. It has been recommended, for example, that a systematic examination of all alloys of metals should be carried out, proceeding from the most simple binary compounds to the more complicated ternary and quaternary ones. But if only thirty of the known metals were operated upon, the number of binary alloys, it is calculated, would be

[1] " Culture demanded by Modern Life," p. 34.

435, of ternary alloys 4,060, of quaternary 27,405, without paying any regard to the varying proportions of the metals. If we varied all the ternary alloys by quantities not less than one per cent., the number of these alloys only would be over 11,000,000. So also in regard to the possible chemical combinations. Taking the number of elements at sixty-one, the number of compounds containing different selections of four elements each would be more than half a million. As the same elements often combine in different proportions, it would hardly be possible to assign any limit to the possible compounds that chemistry can furnish. Under such circumstances, it is inevitable that induction should never give more than incomplete knowledge.[1]

In regard to political science, John Stuart Mill, in his inaugural address, as Rector of the University of St. Andrew's, said: "It is evident, to whoever comes to the study from that of the experimental sciences, that no political conclusions of any value for practice can be arrived at by direct experience. Such specific experience as we can have serves only to verify, and even that insufficiently, the conclusions of reasoning. . . . All true political science is, in one sense of the phrase, *a priori*, being deduced from the tendencies of things, tendencies known either through our general experience of human nature, or as the result of an analysis of the course of history considered as a progressive evolution."

[1] Jevons, vol. i., p. 218.

The same is true of the other sciences, and especially of the great natural laws. The law of gravity, for example, has never been proved by any exhaustive induction. Only a small portion of terrestrial matter, and a few of the myriad stars of heaven, have been tested as conforming to it. The first law of motion that "every body continues in its state of rest or of uniform motion in a straight line, except in so far as it may be compelled by impressed forces to change that state," can never be proved by induction. That a real body should move uniformly in a straight line, is contrary to all observation. It not only has never been seen, but can never be seen. As Lewes says, "No such phenomenon could present itself in a universe like ours, where motion is always accelerated or retarded, and always more or less divergent from a straight line."

The same is true of the conservation of energy. All the inductive proof that can be given of it is only approximative. There is always a certain discrepance between the sum of force we start with in one form, such as heat, and the sum we recover in another form, such as motion. This discrepance, in careful experiments, may be very slight. By still greater care it may be made so infinitesimal that in practice it may be disregarded. But the discrepance is always there, and, however close we may approach to an absolute equivalence, we can never attain it. As Jevons says,[1] "The most that we can do by experi-

---

[1] Vol. ii., p. 83.

ment is, to show that the energy entering into any experimental combination is almost exactly equal to what comes out of it, and the more nearly so, the more exactly we perform all the measurements. Absolute equality is always a matter of assumption." Long before we reach that point, the thread we are tracing grows so fine as no longer to be held by our fingers. Should some minute part of it vanish, we could not detect the loss. The cogency granted to the scientific proof of either the first law of motion, or the conservation of energy, or the indestructibility of matter or force, depends upon the experience that, the farther we extend our observation, the more delicate we make our tests, and exclude disturbing conditions, the nearer we come to the realization of the law.' It is but the same kind of approximative evidence which religion brings to show the benevolence and providence of God. As we understand Nature and human events more and more thoroughly, we find more and more that every thing is good.

The fact is, as Stanley Jevons says,[2] "not one of the inductive truths which men have established, or think they have established, is really safe from exception or reversal. . . . Euler expresses no more than the truth when he says that it would be impossible to fix on any one thing really existing of which we could have so perfect a knowledge as to put us beyond the reach of mistake." Though we have ob-

[1] Jevons, vol. ii., p. 271.
[2] "Principles of Science," vol. i., p. 274.

served ten thousand swans to be white, it does not follow but what the next swan may be black. Though we have observed flame to burn a hundred million times, it does not follow but what the next time it may not—the law ruling it being a change-bearing one, such as Babbage made in one of his calculating-machines, or some unsuspected cause being in existence which may produce a different effect.[1] "The

---

[1] Few, probably, are aware how large a number of examples of these change-bearing laws and exceptions to what has been supposed universal uniformities, have been disclosed by recent science.

The expansion of solids and liquids by heat, and their contraction by cold, is a law so general and intimately connected with the very theory of heat, that it would seem as if a real anomaly to it ought not to be expected. Indeed, for a long time no exception was observed. But modern researches have disclosed the fact that stretched India-rubber and a few other solids contract, instead of expanding, by heat, and that water, though conforming to the usual law from 212° Fahr. down to 39½°, then changes, and from 39½° to its freezing-point expands with the increase of cold.

Again, it is one of the most important and rigorous laws of chemistry that equal volumes of gases exactly correspond to equivalent weights of the substances. Unfortunately, phosphorus and arsenic give vapors exactly twice as dense as they should do by analogy, and mercury and cadmium diverge in the other direction, giving vapors half as dense as we should expect. Physicists assert again, as an absolutely universal law, that in liquefaction heat is absorbed, yet sulphur is, at least, an apparent exception. Until a recent discovery of Mr. Hermann Smith, all our knowledge of rods and strings, plates and membranes, had agreed in the law of isochronism—that, however the amplitude may vary, the times of vibration will be the same. But in the so-called "air-reed," into which the stream of air is moulded in the embouchure of an organ-pipe, an absolute reversal of this is exhibited. (*See Nature*, 1874, vol. x., p. 161.)

A multitude of further similar cases might be quoted. The num-

conclusions of scientific inference," to quote Jevons again,[1] "appear to be always of an hypothetical and purely provisional nature. The best-calculated results which it can give are never absolute probabilities; they are purely relative to the extent of our information. It seems to be impossible for us to judge how far our experience gives us adequate information of the universe as a whole, and of all the forces and phenomena which can have place therein."[2]

To the same effect I may quote, from the opposite side of the philosophical camp, the declarations of Taine and Lewes. Speaking of the laws of real things gained by induction, Taine says: "However well-established and verified one of these laws may be, if we wish to apply it outside of the little circle of space and short fragment of duration to which our observations are limited, it becomes probable only. It is not absolutely certain that the law of gravitation continues to hold good beyond the farthest nebulæ of Herschel. It is not at all certain that, in the sun, oxygen and hydrogen preserve the

---

ber of them, in fact, is so great, that Jevons declares that " it would be easy to point out an almost *infinite* number of other unexplained anomalies."—(" Principles of Science," vol. ii., p. 341.)

[1] " Principles of Science," vol. ii., p. 465.

[2] The passages quoted from Jevons are but two out of a dozen similar passages that might be quoted, in which the merely probable nature of scientific conclusions is emphatically affirmed. (*See* vol. i., pp. 3, 265, 271, 275; vol. ii., pp. 429, 432, 443, 459.)

chemical affinity which we find they have here with us." [1]

"In this assumption," says Lewes, "of an identity amid diversity, this *inference*, that what has been found to coexist with certain characters will be found elsewhere to coexist with similar characters, lies the whole reach of induction. . . . Consequently, induction can never be more than a more or less probable *guess*. It is not knowledge till it ceases to be inductive by the verification of each of its applied inferences." [2]

The Gordian knots of existence not allowing themselves thus to be untied by any complete inductions, they must be severed in some more summary way. Religion does so by its grand hypotheses of God and soul—for they are in a certain sense hypotheses—transcending at first, nay, transcending forever, the sweep of any possible induction. For thus resorting to hypotheses Religion has always been reproached, and it has had commended to it the Baconian method of laborious accumulation of facts, and careful and orderly abstraction from them of general axioms or laws. It has been reminded of Newton's warning against "anticipations." It has been admonished to recall the similar *scholium* of the great philosopher, "Whatever is not deduced from the phenomena is to be called an hypothesis,

---

[1] "On Intelligence," p. 426.
[2] G. H. Lewes's "Problems of Life and Mind," vol. ii., p. 159.

and hypotheses, whether metaphysical or physical, have no place in experimental philosophy." But, in point of fact, it is just this procedure of anticipating Nature, of framing hypotheses, which has yielded all the more lofty and successful results of science. " Those who have most advanced the natural science since Bacon's day," says Prof. Henfrey, "have departed from the rigorous method of induction, and by this alone rendered possible the rapid progress of the sciences." To the same effect, says Prof. Jevons,[1] " whether we look to Galileo and Gilbert, his contemporaries, or to Newton and Descartes, his successors, we find that discovery was achieved by the exactly opposite method to that advanced by Bacon." In spite of Newton's condemnation of hypotheses, "the greater part of his 'Principia,'" says Prof. Jevons, "is purely hypothetical." His practice is the most splendid vindication of their use. Huyghens's brilliant achievements were gained by the same means.

The history of the inductive sciences, to quote the words of Whewell, " is the rise of theories out of facts and the passing of theories into facts." Laplace's, Darwin's, Spencer's great scientific achievements are all hypotheses.[2] Geology, paleontology, archæology, are all built up by hypotheses. These sciences are but the interpretations we have guessed

---

[1] *Fortnightly Review*, 1873, p. 780.
[2] " Tyndall's Fragments of Science," pp. 155–159.

for a few of Nature's infinite hieroglyphics. "Neither induction nor deduction," Auguste Comte himself has said, "would enable us to understand even the simplest phenomena, if we did not often commence by anticipation on the results;" and in his discourse delivered before the British Association in Liverpool, in 1870, Prof. Tyndall has urged upon his scientific comrades the importance of the imagination as the mightiest instrument of physical investigation, and indicates as the organ that is finally to solve the ultimate problems of physics, "spiritual insight." "Bounded and conditioned by coöperant reason," says Tyndall, "imagination becomes the mightiest instrument of the physical discoverer. Newton's passage from a falling apple to a falling moon was at the outset a leap of the imagination. When William Thomson tries to place the ultimate particles of matter between his compass-points, and to apply to them a scale of millimetres, he is powerfully aided by this faculty. And in much that has been recently said about protoplasm and life, we have the outgoings of the imagination guided and controlled by the known analogies of science. In fact, without this power, our knowledge of Nature would be a mere tabulation of coexistences and sequences. We should still believe in the succession of day and night, of summer and winter; but the soul of Force would be dislodged from our universe; causal relations would disappear, and with them that science which is now building the parts of Nature

into an organic whole."[1] It needs hardly to be remarked, that hypotheses, imagination, insight, are
but secular names for the action and faculty which,
under the standard of Religion, are so much scoffed
at as "faith."

4. But scientific faith, it will be said, legitimates
itself by the test of verification. Religious faith
does not. It is the bringing of its doctrines, by
whatever argument supported, whether by intuition,
authority, evidence, analogy, or hypotheses, squarely up to the test of verification as a final and decisive test, that justifies these methods in the hands of
Science. And it is the disuse of this test by Religion
that in her hands renders them suspicious. Now, on
the one hand, Religion, as I shall show further on, is
able to confirm its fundamental propositions by verifications similar to those employed by Science. On
the other hand, the doctrines of science, even those

---

[1] "Fragments of Science," p. 130.

The editor of *The Popular Science Monthly*, for March, 1875,
in answer to a criticism upon Tyndall, for this use of mental pictur-
ing in science, says: "Our writer says that 'Science starts with
observation and experiment;' but the real starting-point is farther
back. A mental representation must be made before it can be
verified. A certain state of things is conceived or put together in
thought, and is called an hypothesis; and then observation and experiment are appealed to, to test the correctness of the representation,
the truthfulness of the mental picture. Science is not merely seeing
with the eye, or fumbling with instruments. Any blockhead can do
these; but it is to reconstruct Nature in thought. . . . To do this
the imagination or image-forming faculty comes into incessant play."
(p. 621.)

generally accepted, are in many cases destitute of any proper verification.

For instance: The fundamental law in pneumatics, that, where gases are allowed to mix, every gas is in a constant state of diffusion of every part into every part, cannot be verified by observation; for in very many if not most cases the portions of gases, or the different gases, cannot be followed and identified. One atom of oxygen, for example, is practically undistinguishable from another atom. Only by keeping a certain volume of gas safely inclosed in a bottle can we assure ourselves of its identity. Allow it to mix with other oxygen, and we have lost all power of identification.

The results of celestial spectroscopy, based as we have seen them to be on analogy, allow no means of verification. For the assumptions underlying them —that substances on celestial bodies vibrate exactly as substances on the earth, and that some different substance, either a known or an unknown one, cannot have synchronous vibrations with the substance observed here to have these vibrations—can never be established. Should either assumption be reasonably suspected to be erroneous, as the last already has been by Prof. Young, from certain phenomena, the whole superstructure would fall with it.

Social science, as John Stuart Mill has pointed out,[1] is incapable of direct verification. The nebular and the development hypotheses, and all the accounts

---

[1] "System of Logic," Book VI., Chapter IX., Sec. 6.

of the past history of the universe, in the astronomical, geological, or biological departments, are incapable of direct verification.[1] None of these events have

[1] In Tyndall's "Belfast Address," he speaks of the provability of the doctrine of evolution as follows: "The strength of the doctrine of evolution consists, not in an experimental demonstration (for the subject is hardly accessible to this mode of proof), but in its general harmony with the method of Nature as hitherto known."

George H. Lewes speaks of the two hypotheses of the origin of life, that of creation and that of natural selection, as follows: "Both these hypotheses of origin must always remain hypotheses. Knowledge of what things are under observed conditions may be absolute; it can never lead to more than hypothetical statements of what things were under other conditions; and since it is manifestly impossible that we should ever know what were the exact conditions under which organic life emerged, we can do no more than guess at origins."—("Problems of Life and Mind," vol. ii., p. 76.)

Still more emphatic is the testimony of Prof. Huxley. Speaking of the animal pedigree assigned to man by Darwin and Haeckel, he says: "It need hardly be said that, in dealing with such a problem as this, Science rapidly passes beyond the bounds of positive, verifiable fact, and enters those of more or less justifiable speculation. But there are very few scientific problems, even of those which have been and are being most successfully solved, which have been or can be approached in any other way.

"Our views respecting the nature of the planets, of the sun and stars, are speculations which are not and cannot be directly verified; that great instrument of research, the atomic hypothesis, is a speculation which cannot be directly verified; the statement that an extinct animal, of which we know only the skeleton, and never can know any more, had a heart and lungs, and gave birth to young which were developed in such and such a fashion, may be one which admits of no reasonable doubt, but it is an unverifiable hypothesis. I may be as sure as I can be of any thing that I had a thought, yesterday morning, which I took care neither to utter nor to write down, but my conviction is an utterly unverifiable hypothesis. So that unverified and

ever been tested by observation, or can ever henceforth be tested by observation. What physicist stood by and saw the glowing gas condense into sun and planets? What *savant* watched the annulosa develop the primordial vertebrate; the amphibia the mammal; the mammal the man? What man of to-day looked on the dry land uniting England with France, or the seas that once covered Wales, the Netherlands, or the larger part of Russia? What scientific enchanter holds the wand that can roll back the wheel of Time to those long-passed epochs? or what experimenter so mighty as to be able to reproduce all those vanished conditions of the universe which gave birth to its primeval phenomena? The only verification possible in any of these great departments is to show that the cause assigned, according to present laws of causation, would account for the phenomena. Not that they did cause them, nor that the laws of causation have come down unchanged, nor even that no other cause could have produced the given effects. The same is true of those important scientific theories, the atomic constitution of chemical substances and the ether-waves[1] which are regarded universally as the vehicle

even unverifiable hypotheses may be great aids to the progress of knowledge, may have a right to be believed with a high degree of assurance." (*See* article, "Darwin and Haeckel," p. 596, POPULAR SCIENCE MONTHLY, March, 1875.)

[1] "The domain in which this motion of light is carried on," says Tyndall, "lies entirely beyond the reach of our senses. The waves of light require a medium for their formation and propagation, but

of light. No verification by any kind of observation is possible.[1] For the most powerful microscope has never discerned a molecule or an atom. They are at least a thousand times smaller, according to Thomson's calculations, than any particle which the microscope can discern. They are as pure assumptions as the vortices of Descartes, or the emitted corpuscles of Newton's theory of light. All the verification that can be given is to show, in the phrase which Tyndall so frequently uses, in his paper on the "Scientific Imagination," that the phenomena occur *as if there were such substrata.* There is nothing to prove that they are *actually* there, or that some other better explanation may not be discovered and banish them, as the belief in emitted corpuscles and imponderable fluids has already been dismissed.

So, again, the truths of geometry, the doctrines of the indestructibility of matter and force, and the uniformity of Nature, all laws claiming universality and absoluteness, as it was before shown that they could not be *proved* by observation, so neither can they be verified by experience, that is, in their universality and absoluteness. Their only verification is approximative and probable.

we cannot see, or feel, or taste, or smell this medium."—(Tyndall's "Fragments of Science," p. 214.)

[1] " It is not pretended that the existence of atoms has been or can be proved or disproved."—(Presidential Address of Prof. Lovering before the American Association at Hartford, 1874.)

Thus is it shown by examination that Science, when she would grasp any of the wider laws and deeper secrets of Nature, must and does employ the very methods for which Religion is rejected, and is open to the same objections. If the one is not to be rejected or doubted because of these, why is the other? If the physicist may rely upon man's natural faith in an external reality, and in the practical veracity of his physical senses, why may not the spiritualist rely upon the same natural faith of mankind, when it declares the inward reality of the soul and the veracity of moral and spiritual discernment? If the scientific world accept the belief in the indestructibility of force as an ultimate belief, not to be questioned, why may not the religious world legitimately receive the natural belief of man in the immortality of the soul as a similar ultimate belief, not to be distrusted? If the student of Nature customarily receives the word of a Newton, a Laplace, or a Tyndall, as presumably to be trusted, even when declaring that which he cannot fully understand, why may not the Christian disciple accept the authority of a superior spiritual discerner, like Jesus Christ, with a similar confidence? If the optician may lawfully deduce from the phenomena of light, that he studies, the hypothesis of an invisible, infinite ether, why may not the theist, with equal justification, infer from the kosmic phenomena, that he studies, the hypothesis of an invisible, infinite Creator and Guardian; and if the one hypothesis is not to be declared a "mere figment of the scientific fancy"[1] because it cannot be directly verified by sense-perception, why is the other to be regarded as a figment of the religious imagination, merely because it lacks the same kind of sense-demonstration?

[1] Tyndall's "Fragments of Science," p. 133.

CHAPTER V.

FAITHS OF SCIENCE—AIMS AND OBJECTS.

THUS it is seen that science rests on the same grounds and employs the same methods which its champions have censured religion for using.

But perhaps it will be said that, although science and religion have no really different grounds or methods, yet the different objects to which they are applied in each justify men in refusing to the propositions of theology the same credit that they give to those of physical inquiry. There is certainly an apparent difference of this kind, seeming to many very real and broad, which ought not to be omitted from any thorough discussion of this subject. An opponent of religion would put it something like this :

Religion, perhaps, may employ the same instrumentalities as science, but the trouble is, she aims to master with them truths which they are not competent to grasp. Science deals with material masses, their relations of heat, color, weight, and their changes of form, bulk, place, quality, etc.—all of them things visible and tangible.

The endeavor of religion, however, is to establish the existence, nature, and relations of immaterial beings, called spirits; a Supreme Spirit behind and above all Nature, and minor spirits within each human body—things which no sense can ever discern.

Science attends to phenomena, their coexistences and successions. It busies itself about those things only of which there is or can be experience. Religion aspires to go behind the empirical to the metempirical. It talks of ideal conceptions and supersensual objects.

Science, again, limits itself to the aspects of things in their relations to us, under the limitations of earthly life, and as they may be clearly comprehended by us. Religion, on the contrary, dreams of the Absolute, the Infinite, the Eternal, and loses itself in the mazes of the contradictory and the inconceivable. Behold in this difference of aims and objects the ample justification of the modern suspicions of religion. Immaterial Spirit, First Cause, Eternal, Infinite, Absolute—how can such things ever be known? What finger ever touched them, what optic or auditory nerve ever gave report of them, what telescope was ever or can ever be made so space-penetrating, what microscope so delicate in its scrutiny as to discern objects of this nature? "They are," says Büchner, "arbitrary assumptions without any real basis." "Human thought and human knowledge," he maintains,[1] are "incapable of discovering or knowing any thing supersensual." "The materialist," says Virchow, "can never be satisfied with it: he knows only bodies and their qualities; what is beyond he terms transcendental, and he considers transcendentalism as an aberration of the human mind."

Indeed, to the physical inquirer, supersensual and immaterial things are not even conceivable. "A force not united to matter, but floating freely above it," Moleschott characterizes as "an ideal notion." The idea of immaterial spirit, Carl Vogt declares to be "a pure hypothesis," and assigns it a place among "speculative fables." "The remark of a somewhat crazy, but all the more ingenious, father of the Church," says the author of the "Old Faith and the New" (p. 152), "has become the principle of modern science—'Naught is immaterial but what is naught.'"

Similarly says Büchner: "Those who talk of a creative power which is said to have produced the world out of nothing are ignorant of the first and most simple principle founded upon experience and the contemplation of Nature. How could a power have existed not manifested in material substance, but governing it arbitrarily according to individual views? Neither could separately existing forces be transferred to chaotic matter, and produce the world

"Force and Matter," p. xli., Introduction.

in this manner; for we have seen that a separate existence of either is an impossibility."[1]

Certainly, say the scientific objectors, it is not for man to comprehend God, for the finite to think to find out the Infinite. All conceptions involving Infinity, Self-Existence, Eternity, Absolute Being (Herbert Spencer labors at length to show, in the second and fourth chapters of his "First Principles," and in other parts of his writings repeats the statement again and again), are but "pseudo-ideas," "symbolic conceptions of the illegitimate order." Every religious system "involves itself in the unthinkable." Every theologian who attempts to tell the nature of God or the soul falls into contradiction and absurdity. All the real knowledge that we can attain to is, that "the power which the universe manifests is utterly inscrutable," a conclusion to which Profs. Huxley and Tyndall give repeated and emphatic amens. "As little in our day, as in the days of Job," says Prof. Tyndall, "can man by searching find this power out."[2] Quoting the reply of Napoleon, when, to the *savants* who tried to account for the universe without any Divine agency, raising his finger to the heavens, he said, "It is all very well, gentlemen, but who made all these?" Prof. Tyndall says:[3] "As far as I can see, there is no quality in the human intellect which is fit to be applied

---

[1] "Force and Matter," chapter i.
[2] Address before the British Association, Belfast, 1874.
[3] Fragments of Science," p. 93.

to the solution of the problem. It entirely transcends us. The phenomena of matter and force lie within our intellectual range, and as far as they reach we will, at all events, push our inquiries, but behind and above and around the real mystery lies unsolved, and as far as we are concerned is incapable of solution."

Now, the defender of religion would not deny that there are mysteries insoluble both to religion and science. He would not deny that we must, from the nature of the case, remain ever in ignorance of much, probably of most, that relates to the origin and history of the universe, the character, nature, laws, and relations of God and the soul. But he claims that, though we cannot know all, though we cannot know any thing, perhaps, with absolute certainty, yet we can know something with strong probability—probability equal to that with which men are satisfied in the realm of science. Human intellect cannot, of course, fathom to the bottom the depths of spirit. It cannot comprehend all the mysteries of the Divine. But it can drop the plummet of thought deep enough to know whether that which it is dealing with is matter, such as we know, or something else. It can trace out a section of the Infinite hyperbola sufficient to show whether the curve runs by chance or by law, whether its course is toward the irrational or the rational, toward the evil or the good, toward matter or toward spirit. And narrow as the circle of warrantable belief may be in comparison with the vast sea of the unknowable encircling and confining it, yet Science no more than Religion confines her credence to the sphere of the senses, the circle of the material, or the range wherein nothing inconceivable or contradictory is met with. To claim that in this respect there is any substantial difference between science and religion is a most unfounded pretension. For it can be shown, here as before, that Science is in the same box as Religion, and shoots her arrows at just as transcendental targets.

First, Science no more than Religion restricts its belief to what it can see, hear, touch, smell, feel. No more than its rival does it accept the horizon of sense as commensurate with the possibilities of knowledge or existence.

The illustrations of this in the circle of the sciences are countless. If human knowledge had been, as Büchner maintains it is, incapable of attaining to any thing supersensual, its attainments would have been comparatively meagre. Take the most familiar instructions of science, and half of them are things which, if appearance before the bar of the senses is to be taken as the test of credence, would have to be disbelieved. It is a fundamental law in the science of projectiles, for example, that a rifle-ball or cannon-shot, discharged from the gun, describes in its flight a parabola. Yet, what physical observer has followed out with his physical eye the tracing of that curve through the air from the

6

cannon's mouth to the point where it fell, so as exactly to observe or verify it ? Again, probably no man of science doubts that our earth has poles—points, that is, at the extreme north and at the extreme south of our globe, so differently situated from all other points on the globe that an observer there would find his sight of sun and stars unaffected by that daily revolution that, in every man's past experience, wherever he may have been, hourly shifts the apparent position of the heavenly bodies. Here is a most singular phenomenon, opposed to men's daily experience, yet held as an unquestioned part of science.' Nevertheless, no human eye has ever beheld these spots, or is ever likely to behold them. No astronomer, again, has ever seen the other side of the moon. Yet shall we hesitate to believe that it has one ? No chemist has ever seen, grasped, tasted, or smelt, pure oxygen. Even when Andrews compressed it to the density of water, it still remained colorless to the eye, tasteless to the tongue, odorless to the nose, ungraspable by the hand, manifesting itself only by its gravitative, repulsive, chemic, or other forces. Shall we consign, therefore, to the limits of non-existence what constitutes eight-ninths of water, one-half of the earth's crust, and three-fourths of organized beings ?

People in general may be forgiven for thinking that the senses are capable of detecting all that exists. But the thorough scientist is just the man who best knows, or ought to know, how comparatively small a part of the universe of things the senses can catch a glimpse of. He has scientifically measured them and taken the gamut of their power. With the sirene he counts the vibrations of audible sound, and finds that the ordinary ear can hear no note less than fifteen vibrations a second nor more than forty-two thousand. Below or above this limit there is silence to the human ear, yet he does not believe that the vibration of the air ceases, or would be inaudible to an auditory organ of wider compass. With the prism he untwists the rays of the solar beam, and by delicate processes measures their velocity. Only those whose rates exceed three hundred and ninety-nine billion vibrations a second, or fall below eight hundred and thirty-one billion,[1] are visible to the eye. Yet the man of science does not regard the vibrations as ceasing beyond these limits. When at the extreme red end of the spectrum they cease to be visible, the thermometer and the thermopyle still detect them by their heat, and beyond the extreme violet the phenomena of fluorescence or photo-chemical action disclose them as chemical force. "The light-giving rays from any object are only a fraction," says Tyndall, "of the total radiation." In the electric light, for instance, they constitute no more than one-ninth.[2]

There are thus sounds to which we are deaf, light to which we are blind, heat, magnetism, elec-

[1] Herschel's "Familiar Lectures," p. 312.
[2] "Fragments of Science," p. 206.

tricity to which we are insensible. A thousand forms of force strike us hourly, and our dull nerves know it not. A thousand objects and motions envelop us, and the narrow boundaries of our organs fail to take them in. It was in the belief that there was a vast deal more to see than the naked eye could discern, that physical investigators with infinite ingenuity and patience have contrived instruments for magnifying the invisible, until it was brought within the scope of sense.

And their faith has been well rewarded. In what seemed the blank darkness of the heavens there have been revealed to them suns and nebulæ, planets and attendant moons. In what seemed a simple, unoccupied drop of water, there has been disclosed a host of both organic and inorganic bodies, the plants as actively moving as the animals, and the mineral particles dancing about with as incessant motion as if alive. In the last half-century the men of science have seen telescope and microscope continually increased in power, and other instruments, equally wonderful in widening the realm of observation, invented and improved, and never have they found increased power fail to discover beyond the former limit of perception still more phenomena.

Suppose these instruments still further increased, no matter how much, and who doubts that still new sights, now undiscernible, would open before us? Or suppose that human ingenuity should de-

vise telescopes and microscopes for the ear, for the
sense of taste, smell, or touch, and who doubts that
facts before imperceptible by any sense would become revealed to us? The very possibility, however, of such greater victories of sense implies real
and knowable existence beyond the grasp of present sense.

In their own field of inquiry, physicists freely
assert this. Tyndall justly speaks of " that region
inaccessible to sense, which embraces so much of
the intellectual life of the physical investigator."

De La Rive ascribed the haze of the Alps to
floating organic germs; and the advocates of the
germ theory of disease and the opponents of spontaneous generation maintain, as their basic fact, the
profuse existence in common air of such living
germs, pelting us every moment, yet unfelt and unseen. Whether or not such infinitesimal organic
germs exist, yet we have in the atmosphere," says
Tyndall,[1] " particles that defy both the microscope
and the balance, which do not darken the air, and
which exist, nevertheless, in multitudes sufficient to
reduce to insignificance the Israelitish hyperbole regarding the sands upon the sea-shore."

To identify what the microscope fails to see
with the non-existent, Prof. Tyndall deems so grave
an error as to take pains to caution biologists against
it. " When, for example, the contents of a cell are
described as perfectly homogeneous, as absolutely

[1] "Fragments of Science," p. 151.

structureless, because the microscope fails to distinguish any structure, then, I think the microscope begins to play a mischievous part," and he proceeds to point out, in regard to the profound and complex changes of structure which occur when water is frozen or polarized, that absolutely none of them can be discerned by the microscope. "The causes in which similar conditions hold," he adds, "are simply numberless. Have the diamond, the amethyst, and the countless other crystals formed in the laboratories of Nature and of man no structure? Assuredly they have; but what can the microscope make of it? Nothing."[1]

From the mineralogist and biologist, turn to the chemist. Ask him if he makes the limit of the senses, even when widened to the utmost range to which the most delicate instruments can push it, the limit, in his belief, of real existence or knowledge—and what must be his honest answer? To show you how the whole of chemistry, as a systematized science, is based upon the existence of the molecule and the atom. When the chemist deals with his various substances, he meets such problems as these: How can a body dilate and contract, be melted, vaporized, or solidified? What puts a limit to the process of attenuation? Why do chemical substances unite only in definite proportions? And the result to which he is brought is that a body, such as a grain of salt, is not a simple compact body, but an aggre-

[1] " Fragments of Science," pp. 152, 153.

gation of minute corpuscles, which he calls molecules, and these molecules, in their turn, a group of still smaller and simpler particles, called atoms. The aggregate formed by these particles seems to our senses solid, continuous, and motionless, yet in reality neither its molecules nor its atoms are in contact, nor remain a single minute at rest. By a certain repulsive power, each atom holds itself off from too close proximity to its neighbor. By a certain attractive power it draws toward it such atoms as it has an affinity for, disengages them from other groups, and brings them into league with itself. Through the play of their mutual forces, the atoms are marshaled in just the right number into a certain order or position. With ceaseless oscillations all these atoms are swinging to and fro, circling around some point of equilibrium. Send a current of electricity through the midst of them, and their path becomes more or less elliptic ; put them under the influence of a magnet, and they assume a peculiar helicoidal motion in varying planes. Apply heat, and the vibrations become ampler and more rapid. Increase the heat, and they leave their circular paths and fly off tangentially, moving rectilineally through space. Atoms clash against atoms, rebound, and with ceaseless impact cannonade whatever object would hem them in. Joule calculated the velocity of this atomic bombardment, and found that the boasted guns of modern warfare are unable to compete with it. Sir William Thomson has estimated their size, and set down the maximum distance of the chemical atoms in molecules as the ten-millionth part of one-twenty-fifth of an inch. Other mathematicians have computed their weights and energies. The things which naturally give to us the highest conception of force and majesty are the grand bodies that march so ceaselessly through the heavens, the tidal movement of oceans from end to end of the globe, or the fall of huge masses under the power of gravity ; but all this energy is as nothing in comparison with that which is found to lie in the atoms. It is the nature and force of the atoms that give its shape to the crystal, its quality to the acid or alkali, their color, odor, softness, or hardness to substances. It is the atoms that build up every individual body from a drop of water to a whirling sun.

Now, of all this, the accepted basis of theoretical chemistry and thermodynamics, how much can be produced before the bar of the senses? Of these units of matter, how many have been isolated, separately weighed, measured, or touched? Not a single one. Of these ceaseless motions, how much has been felt or seen? Of these constant clashes, how much has been heard? None at all. If the microscope was not delicate enough to discern the particles which give the azure to the sky, or the infusorial germ which disseminates an epidemic, how far beyond its power of detection must be these atoms, thousands of which are needed to make

the smallest of those bodies? Prof. Tyndall, allud-
ing to Sir William Thomson's studies upon the molecular process involved in the magnetic polarization of light, has said[1] that, "while dealing with
this question, he lived in a world of matter and
motion, to which the microscope has no passport,
and in which it can afford no aid." That must
be the case with every one who would learn any
thing of either molecule or atom. Nevertheless,
the scientific world believes in them, talks of them,
and uses them, not only in its theoretical reasonings,
but in its practical applications and current instructions.

If it receives its warrant from no sense, whence,
then, does it derive its belief in these imperceptible
workers, everywhere present and active—these invisible kings governing Nature by eternal laws?
Evidently from just such mental apprehensions
and inferences as assure religion of God and the
soul.

We have tracked scientific faith beyond the
farthest ken of the microscope to the infinitesimal
mote, beyond the mote to the molecule, beyond the
molecule to the still minuter, more undiscernible
atom. Does scientific faith here at length make a
halt and refuse to go farther? Ask optics, and
hear for its answer its report of the existence, as it
believes, of a substance still more tenuous and im-
palpable, still farther beyond any possible discern-

[1] "Fragments of Science," p. 153.

ment by any sense. In the time of Newton, light was looked upon as a subtile kind of matter emitted from luminous bodies, and shot out upon the senses. The interplanetary and interstellar spaces were voids, merely traversed by these minute missiles. But serious objections, arising from the peculiar phenomena of refraction, interference, and polarization of light successively presented themselves. To explain these, natural philosophers were led to the theory that the motions of light were those of vibration, not of translation. But where there are vibrations, there must be something to vibrate. Physics, therefore, filled again the whole universe with a something which it called ether, which might serve as the vehicle of the luminous waves. This ether, it is believed, surrounds every particle, penetrates every body, fills all space. The hardest iron is not impervious to it. The most complete atmospheric vacuum, even the desert voids that reign between star and star, are full of it, and the absence of common matter only serves to transmit the better the ethereal waves. A ray of light passing from the sun to the earth is a column of ether in vibration. Along it run countless waves, from thirty thousand to seventy thousand in a single inch, and with such amazing velocity that trillions of them enter the eye in the briefest glance at any object. The atoms which it bathes obey it docilely, like balls floating upon the water, rising and falling with its waves. Round their centre of rest they swing in little orbits, now longer, now smaller, now circular, now elliptical. At every point this ether exerts forces of enormous intensity. Sir John Herschel has calculated that its power of resistance to pressure (and conversely its own possible pressure on objects that resist it) is upward of seventeen billions of pounds,[1] and that the intensity of the coercive force called into action in the excitement of a luminous vibration must be thirty thousand million times that of gravity.[2] In comparison with the bulk of this ether, ordinary matter forms but a very trifling part of the universe. For, even if we disregard the ether diffused through ordinary matter and interplanetary spaces, and suppose the whole of our solar system filled with ordinary matter, the proportion between it and the ethereal sphere whose radius is the distance of the nearest fixed star would be only as one to eleven trillions.

And now, if we inquire, again, what warrant from experience has Science for believing in the luminous ether, our answer is as before—none. Though the medium of vision, it and its vibrations are farther beyond all visibleness than the tiniest molecule. Though more tenacious than steel, we move through it constantly without feeling it. Though so enormous is its pressure, no balance can weigh it. Though touching us on every side every second, no touch of ours can detect it. As Prof. Tyndall[3] has

[1] "Familiar Lectures," p. 282.   [2] Ibid., p. 315.
[3] "Fragments of Science," p. 215.

himself said, " the domain in which this motion of light is carried on lies entirely beyond the reach of our senses. The waves of light require a medium for their formation and propagation, but we cannot see or feel or taste or smell this medium. How, then, has its existence been established? By showing that by the assumption of this wonderful, intangible ether all the phenomena of optics are accounted for with a fullness, and clearness, and conclusiveness, which leave no desire of the intellect unfulfilled."

But if science may accept the perception and satisfaction of the reason as good proof of what no observation can discover, why should religion be debarred a similar privilege?

" All that we see of the world," says Pascal, " is but an imperceptible scratch in the vast range of Nature." "And the claim of mere experimentalism," Papillon well adds, " is that it may sentence men to the fixed and stubborn contemplation of this mere scratch."

So far from phenomena comprising all that we can know, the truth is that phenomena give only the lowest grade of knowledge, and the highest is that which most transcends phenomena. Prof. Huxley,[1] speaking of Auguste Comte's " Positive Philosophy," says that the word " positive," " as implying a system of thought which assumes nothing beyond the content of observed facts, implies that which never

---

[1] " Lay Sermons," p. 161.

did exist and never will." The outward and visible
phenomena are but the raw material of knowledge,
or, to use the expression of Tyndall,[1] " the counters
of the intellect," " and our science," as he goes on
to say, " would not be worthy of its name and fame,
if it halted at facts, however practically useful, and
neglected the laws which accompany and rule phenomena."

The first step in science, then, is, to group facts
about some thought. Then these first classifications
must be illuminated by some more general conception ; and if a science is to be developed to the highest grade these general conceptions must be synthe-
sized in some law of its laws—some one grand idea
summing it all up. What the physical inquirer thus
pursues amid his retorts, his herbariums, mineralogi-
cal cabinets, or zoölogical museums, is ideas ; and in
the present state of science there is nothing more
remarkable than the ideal nature of its results. We
have seen this already in regard to chemistry and
optics. If we look at geometry we find it to be
throughout a work of mental construction, grounded
upon and guided by pure mental insight of space,
and reasonings therefrom. Had geometrical truths
required for acceptance phenomenal demonstration,
we should not have known a single proposition. An
exact right angle has no existence as a phenomenon,
a perfect sphere is impossible as a fact.

Arithmetic and algebra, similarly, are ideal con-

[1] "Fragments of Science," p 227.

structions built up from the metaphysical conception of number. It may be said that the idea of number is simply borrowed from the phenomenal world. But, as we have it, and use it, it is stripped thoroughly of concrete objectivity, and reduced to simple relations between symbolic objects. If number be altogether a teaching of experience, where did experience observe its two poles—zero and infinity?

In astronomy, resting as it does on geometry and arithmetic, there is necessarily the same idealness. Kepler's laws of planetary action, and Newton's laws of motion, are not laws of fact, but types of the scientific imagination. The postulates of the astronomer, uniform velocity and elliptical motion, have no place in exact reality. The same is true of that which the science of mechanics rests on—uniform force and rectilineal motion. No eye has seen or shall see it. So, again, in electricity, magnetism, thermodynamics, the subtile analyses of modern investigators have banished altogether the former theories of material fluids, and substituted the conception of invisible forces. The scientific energies now believed in are not physical things, but mental data. Gravity, for example, is not a material entity, but the correlate of thought to motion, the occult cause inferred by the mind where change of place is observed. The fact, in fine, is, as George H. Lewes[1] has said, "Were the whole circle of the sciences to pass before us, each would in turn display the essen-

---

[1] "Problems of Life and Mind," p. 271.

tially ideal nature of its construction," and again, in his " Philosophy of Aristotle" (p. 66), " The fundamental ideas of modern science are as transcendental as any of the axioms in ancient philosophy."

If transcendentalism be justifiable with science, why should it be an aberration of mind with religion ? If the inability of sense to discern many of the things that science believes in is no bar to a valid knowledge of material things, why should it disprove the existence of spiritual things?

Because, perhaps the man of science may here respond, because all things that science believes really to exist, though in some cases not such as can be actually observed, owing to the weakness of our senses, are always conceivably so. Imagine our powers of observation sufficiently increased, and they would become visible and tangible. They belong to the realm of matter and its qualities; the quantity of matter may be very attenuated, but it is matter still. Whatever ideal constructions science uses are derived from material phenomena, and are reducible again to it, or translatable in terms of body and its functions, or, if not, are recognized as mere fictions, convenient for calculation or statement, but not regarded as things actually existing. To use the recent distinction which Lewes has proposed, science is often metaphysical, but never metempirical ; it accepts the extra-sensible but not the super-sensible. All that is immaterial is, in the view of science, non-existent.

Were these statements true, there certainly would exist here an essential difference between the objects of religion and those of science. It may be venturesome to deny them, but it does not seem to me that they are valid. Science, it seems to me, in many points, implies at least, if it does not directly recognize, the existence of the immaterial.

All the objects that science studies are seen in space. All the events that it traces are known as occurring in time. These two, space and time, are fundamental conditions of all science. Yet neither space nor time is itself a material thing. The extension of a body, the duration of a motion or change, are, to be sure, qualities of material things. But the space which receives and incloses all extended matter, the time which is the ground of all succession or duration, these are not even conceivably to be seen or heard or felt, not even conceivably to be regarded as substances, however infinitely attenuated. Sense may tell us of the finite extension of an individual object, but sense has never and can never tell us of the Infinite Space which the apprehension of each particular extension presupposes. From experience we may learn of the order and duration of particular occurrences. But from experience we cannot learn of the Eternal Time which is the implied condition of all temporal events. Shall space and time, then, be set down as fictions of the intellect? That equally is impossible without destroying the whole edifice of knowledge. For their existence is involved in the existence of every object and property of the actual world.

The existence of what is immaterial seems to be involved, again, in any satisfactory explanation of the dynamics of Nature. How, for example, if we suppose no other kind of force in existence than that which is a property of material objects and seated in them, can the attraction of gravitation, cohesion and adhesion, the repulsion of heat, the occurrence of both attractive and repulsive forces in magnetism and electricity, be explained? Immense voids separate planet from planet, star from star. Yet the force of gravitation almost instantly passes from one to the other. Great intervals may separate two electric currents, or a magnet from a magnetic body; and yet the electric or magnetic force will act from one to the other. For example, it is now considered proved that the sun acts upon the earth as a magnet. Even between molecule and molecule similar interspaces exist. In the hardest of substances, the scientific men tell us, the molecules are not in contact with their neighboring molecules. Were they so, bodies would be absolutely incompressible. The fact is, however, that there is no body that is not more or less compressible. Those that are but slightly compressible by the most powerful mechanical means, contract or interpenetrate under the force of chemical affinity. Sulphuric acid and water, though not sensibly yielding to pressure, yet, when mixed, give a resulting volume considerably less than the aggregate volume of the two liquids used. According to Faraday we may cast into potassium its equivalent of oxygen, and again both oxygen and hydrogen in a twofold number of atoms, and yet, with all these additions, the matter shall become less and less till it is not two-thirds of its original volume. A space which would be filled by four hundred and thirty atoms of potassium may thus be made to contain seven hundred of potassium and twenty-one hundred of oxygen and hydrogen.

Such experiments make it evident that considerable interspaces separate even the nearest atoms. Now, if there be no force except that which is a quality of some material body, and seated in it, how can these various forms pass beyond the periphery of their respective material seats, traverse these void spaces, and act upon other bodies at a distance?

Is it conceivable that a material body can, through its strictly material force, act where it does not exist, or where no medium intervenes through which to transmit its force? Let the great discoverer of gravitation answer. "It is inconceivable," says Newton, in a celebrated passage of his letter to Bentley, " that inanimate brute matter should, without the mediation of something else, which is not material, operate upon and affect other matter without mutual contact. . . . That gravity should be innate, inherent, and essential to matter, so that one body may act upon another through a vacuum, without the mediation of any thing else, by and through which their action and force may be conveyed from one to the other, is to me so great an absurdity that I believe no man, who in philosophical matters has a competent faculty of thinking, can ever fall into it."

Or, if more modern authority is desired, the recent and weighty words of Prof. Challis[1] and Prof. Maxwell may be quoted :

" There is no other kind of force than pressure by contact of one body with another. . . . The rule of philosophy which makes personal sensation and experience the basis of scientific knowledge . . . forbids recognizing any other mode of moving a body than this. When, therefore, a body is caused to move without apparent contact and pressure of another body, it must still be concluded that the pressing body, although invisible, exists, unless we are prepared to admit that there are physical operations which are and ever will be incomprehensible to us. . . . All physical force being pressure, there must be a medium by which the pressure is exerted."

" If something," says Prof. Clerk Maxwell,[2] " is transmitted from one particle to another at a distance, what is its condition after it has left the one particle and before it has reached the other ? If this something is the potential energy of the two particles, how are we to conceive this energy as existing in a point of space coinciding neither with the one

---

[1] *Philosophical Magazine,* vol. xxxii., § 4, p. 467.
[2] " Electricity and Magnetism," vol. ii., p. 437.

particle nor the other? In fact, whenever energy is transmitted from one body to another in time, there must be a medium or substance in which the energy exists."

Suppose, then, in order that we may interpret gravitation and the other attractive forces as material forces, we boldly diffuse through all the vast regions where they are displayed, between star and star, between molecule and molecule, an invisible intervening medium, bathing them on all sides, and pressing them one toward another. Suppose we say, as Prof. Challis does, that the luminous ether presents to us, as actually existing, such an omnipresent, ever-pressing medium, and that the vibratory motion of atoms or larger material bodies in the midst of this sea of ether is sufficient, in accordance with Prof. Guthrie's famous experiments, and Sir William Thomson's calculations, to direct the ethereal pressure upon gravitative, cohesive, or magnetic centres. Still the difficulty is not overcome. To interpret gravitation thus, as transmission of pressure through the luminiferous ether, seems inconsistent with the instant, or almost instant, action of gravitation through the greatest distances. The velocity of light through the ether, though exceedingly swift, yet occupies quite an appreciable time—several minutes in passing from planet to planet, and years in going from star to star. But the velocity of gravitation, if any finite measure can be given to it, is at least, according to Laplace's calculations, fifty millıon times that of light. Moreover, if attraction be a result of ethereal pressure, what is there without the ether to press it thus ever inward? or, if there is nothing, what prevents it, as Sir John Herschel asked, from expanding into infinite space, and losing itself there? Is it conceivable that this ether, any more than other matter, should be free from all discontinuity, all division into constituent parts and intervals between them? If not, then the existence of such an unbroken, continuous substance, penetrating all bodies and filling all the interstices of grosser matter, and acting as the transmitting medium to the forces of bodies, ought to make all solids and liquids transparent to light, heat, and electricity. Such a medium ought not, at least, to be both a conductor and a non-conductor of electricity, both transparent and opaque to light, both a heat-transmitter and a heat-absorbent.

Again, if the ether has no void spaces anywhere in it, then it must absolutely fill space full. How, then, is any of that motion of which all Nature is full, and which the materialists tell us constitutes all varieties of force, possible? If a body is to move with momentum, so as to give a shock, there must be space for it to move through. Before it can move at all, there must be a free space for it to move into. If it pushes weaker matter away to make room for itself, then there must be free space for that weaker matter to move into. If all space be already full, motion is impossible. Theoretically,

then, the ether cannot be destitute of void intervals
between its parts; and, in point of fact, physicists
regard it, like all other matter, as composed of its
separate ethereal atoms, situated at distances which,
in proportion to the size of the ether-atom, are fully
as great as, if not vastly greater than, the intervals of
common matter. Subtile, then, as is the hypothesis
of an omnipresent ethereal medium, pressing all
matter together, the difficulty of action at a distance
remains undiminished.

If the leaping of force over the ninety-two million miles of celestial space that separates the sun from
the earth requires either an intervening medium
through which it may act, or some other interpretation of it than as transmission of material motion or
pressure or other quality seated in matter, equally
does the passage over the minutest atomic interval;
and, as we cannot go on forever imagining finer
and finer media—as we must somewhere leave the
room that will give opportunity for motion—ought
we not frankly to accept the opposite alternative—
the acceptance of force as something capable of acting, and therefore existing where matter does not
exist, as, in fine, an immaterial principle?

Perhaps it may be said that Le Sage's famous
hypothesis, which Sir William Thomson recently re-
suscitated, is sufficient to explain gravitation and all
other kinds of attractive force without supposing
any thing else than motions and qualities of matter.
This hypothesis supposes that an infinity of atoms

fly with excessive velocity through all mundane regions, inward bound from the immensity of ultra-mundane space. Ceaselessly pelting all objects on all sides, the result is that any two objects at a certain distance apart will, in reference to each other, be mutually screened from this bombardment on the faces looking toward each other, and will thus be reciprocally attracted. This is certainly the boldest, the most ingenious, the most purely mechanical of all explanations of attractive force. But, leaving unnoticed its pure hypotheticalness and transcendence of all possible experience, this theory but removes its difficulties to other points. Whence is derived this celestial storm? We must go outside the world of stars for that. On this theory, as on that of Challis,[1] "the universe is not even temporarily automatic, but must be fed from moment to moment by an agency external to itself." The drawing together of bodies may possibly be explained by the pressure of such an atomic hailstorm; but it presents no explanation of what is equally inconsistent with any interpretation of force as a transmission of material motion or pressure, namely, the repulsive powers exhibited by gases, and by solids and fluids when heated, magnetized, or electrified. Moreover, it brings us squarely up against another form of physical force, explicable only as an immaterial principle. I mean the force of elasticity. If these invisible pelting atoms be hard and inelastic,

---

[1] *American Journal of Science and Arts*, October, 1874, p. 306.

then every time they strike a body they must lose some of their energy. As Sir John Herschel[1] says, "in the collision of inelastic bodies, *vis viva* is necessarily and invariably destroyed. . . . Taking such a system in its entirety (where force exists not), there is no possibility of its reproduction. . . . Such an arrangement must of necessity be rapidly self-destructive, and must result in the gradual but speedy dying away of all relative motion."

In order, then, that the system of Nature be conceived as permanent, in order that our theory may harmonize with the observed constancy of the physical forces, the atoms must be capable of so rebounding that after a collision they shall have the same velocity as before. This Sir William Thomson perceived, and in his reconstruction of Le Sage's theory employed as materials, not hard atoms, but molecules of perfect elasticity.

But whence is this elasticity obtained, and what is the nature of elastic force? This is an inquiry, important not only in this connection, but for any adequate explanation of all those numerous phenomena, in solids, in fluids, especially in gases, in which elasticity is involved. Take a gas, for example, which presses on all sides upon the envelope containing it. The mechanical explanation of this is, that the gas is constituted of material particles which move in all possible directions, each in a right line, and which change direction without change of ve-

[1] "Familiar Lectures," pp. 465, 466.

locity where they meet a fixed obstacle. The pressure of the gas is due to the shocks of the gaseous molecules against the containing walls. Now, such an inclosed gas, if left in an hermetical vessel, does not gradually lose its force of pressure till it becomes nothing, but retains it undiminished. This simple fact implies that the gaseous molecules, when they strike their containing walls or collide with one another, as they are continually doing, rebound with the same velocity with which they struck. We say this is because the gaseous molecules possess elastic force, and imagine the matter explained. But let us follow out in thought the course of a molecule when it strikes an obstacle and rebounds, and we may not, perhaps, be so easily satisfied. First, upon the occurrence of a collision, the molecule loses all its own velocity, it comes to a dead halt for an infinitely short instant, and then it regains an equal velocity in a contrary direction. We see, then, that to effect this, there must be something which is capable, first, of destroying established movement; then, when the body has been brought to a state of repose, starting it again with a velocity equal to what it had before. What, then, is the nature of this something, possessed of so great and unique a power? Does it reside in the material atom as one of its properties? Let us compress our gas, observe the relation of its temperature under compression to the degree of compression, and we shall have a crucial test which will tell us whether the material atoms are elastic

7

and variable in volume or not. If the atoms themselves are elastic and variable in volume, then the gas, the sum of them, may be compressed without increasing the atomic motion, that is, the heat in the gas; and after compression the atoms may expand without requiring any expenditure of atomic motion or thermal energy. But if the atoms be not themselves elastic or variable in volume, then compression of the gas signifies a lessening of the atomic intervals, and consequently a greater atomic velocity or heat, and the reëxpansion of the gas would require the expenditure again of this atomic motion to restore the atoms to their previous stations.

The opposite results of the two hypotheses are then clear. Equally clear is the decisive answer of all thermodynamical experiments, that there is no compression without a corresponding production of heat, and no expansion of a compressed body against pressure without the expenditure of heat. The whole science of thermodynamics rests on the definite and constant correlation of work and heat, and is incompatible with variability of volume in the atoms.[1]

Can the elastic rebound, then, be the result in each case of some anterior motion, in accordance with the view of these pure materialists who would hold as a first law, "no motion without anterior motion?" The sufficient answer is that, in the case

[1] *See* "Conséquences de la Thermodynamique," par G. A. Hirn, p. 208.

of the elastic rebound, the resilient motion is separated from all previous motion by an instant, infinitely short, perhaps, but still an actual instant of rest, during which the direction of movement is reversed. The difficulty cannot be escaped.

Suppose, even, we say that the atom, like an ivory ball, changes its form upon collision with an object, that it is composed of component parts, and that an internal vibratory movement of them is set up, in consequence of which the atom first seeks to regain its old form, and next, this internal motion, passing into translatory motion, the whole atom rebounds—the difficulty is only transferred from the whole atom to the component particles or atoms of the atom. Whence the tendency of one of these particles to return to its place? What is the force that, when it has swung to its farthest limit and stops then for its infinitesimal second of rest, starts it from rest into motion? No anterior motion can explain this, for between the anterior and the posterior motion is always this intervening moment of rest.[1]

If, as Du Bois-Reymond says, and as is logically required by the very conception of it, " the properties of matter can neither be extended outside of itself nor transferred to other material objects," then they are plainly unequal to explaining the phenomena of elasticity as well as those of attraction

[1] " Conséquences de la Thermodynamique," par G. A. Hirn, livre ii., chapitre i.

and repulsion. To explain adequately these fundamental, constant, and ubiquitous properties of Nature, we must conceive force, not as the materialists tell us we can alone properly conceive it, as "the property inseparable from and eternally inherent in matter," as "a motion arising from some previous motion and acting through bodily contact or intervening medium," but as the very reverse of that— as a power which does not depend on anterior motion, which can exist and act where no material medium is present—in short, as an immaterial principle. But if Science can find explanation of many of its most fundamental phenomena only in such a principle, why should it be called "a speculative fable" when presented by the religious thinker? If even in physical relations the difficulties in getting along without supposing the immaterial are greater than the difficulty of supposing it, why in spiritual relations, also, may not it be credited as being something more than "naught?"

But the beliefs of religion, it will be replied, are directed to that which it is not merely difficult to know, but which it is impossible to know—something which is absolutely inconceivable. All our knowledge is relative, that is, a knowledge of a thing through its relations and contrasts with something else. How, then, can we know the Absolute, the One Supreme, existing in and by himself? All our knowledge is of appearances and through the senses. How, then, can we know that which is said to lie beyond appearances, and is certainly inaccessible to the senses—spirit?

Man, and all that belongs to him, is finite. He passes his few fleeting days, indeed, as a pigmy, in a little corner of the universe. Even in his brightest achievements his powers are narrowly limited. There is nothing infinite either in his experiences or in his nature. How, then, can he conceive the Infinite? If, even in imagination, he seek to follow out any mode of the infinite, he ever falls short—no matter how immense his mental flight— within the bounds of the finite. Were it possible to follow through in thought an infinite whole, an infinite time would be required for the operation. Theologians may talk glibly of soul and over-soul, creator and creation, absolute and infinite; they may fancy that they understand them; but they are only deceiving themselves, mistaking familiarity with words for a genuine understanding of things. Their high-sounding terms are but covers to their real ignorance. The realities themselves, if there are realities here, are mysteries beyond all comprehension. The endeavor to conceive of any of them is, as Strauss says of the idea of a Creator, but "merely dealing with an idle phantasy." This is no trumped-up objection, due to the envy of Science. It is a difficulty which metaphysicians and theologians themselves have recognized and stated, a difficulty which beset the path of the most ancient thinkers, which has been affirmed by the acutest

intellects of modern times, such as Pascal, Kant,
Hamilton, and Mansel, and which is fatal to the
claims of religion. Valid knowledge is to be found
only by confining ourselves strictly to that realm
to which Science limits herself—the realm of the
conceivable, that is, of the relative and the phenomenal.

Let us see how this is. It is, indeed, the common aim of Science to keep within the field, not of
phenomena, for we have seen that its highest triumphs are in the regions above phenomena, but of
that which can be readily demonstrated and verified,
and which can be clearly comprehended. And superficial observers, who notice only the exactness of
its measurements, the constancy and regularity of its
laws, the rigor of its demonstrations, generally fancy
it a realm absolutely free from all mysteries. But
the genuine *savant*, who is not content with the regis-
tration of facts, but would know what at bottom is
their significance and explanation, knows science to
be a region of very different character, full of puz-
zling perplexities and marvelous hypotheses, thick
set with dilemmas that land him in the inconceivable, and with problems that have to be given up as
insoluble. "If you wish to be initiated into the
interior of physics," says Novalis, "you must be
initiated into the mysteries of poetry." No flight
of dramatist's fancy is wilder than some of the
sober theories of mathematicians. And, the more
we investigate Nature, the more miracles we find

before our eyes. As Stanley Jevons[1] well says:
" Scientific method must begin and end with the
laws of thought, but it does not follow that it will
save us from encountering inexplicable, and, at
least, apparently contradictory results. . . . Science
does nothing to reduce the number of strange things
that we may believe. When fairly pursued it makes
large drafts upon our powers of comprehension and
belief."

There is no force, for example, better established
scientifically than the force of gravity. Yet it involves the greatest inconceivabilities. It possesses,
in the first place, a velocity almost, if not actually,
instantaneous. It must act through vacuous space ;
if not vacuous interstellar space, yet vacuous atomic
intervals. Not only does it thus act where there is
no intervening medium, but, more perplexing still,
in perfect indifference to all intervening obstacles.
Light, in spite of its velocity and the etherealness
of its medium, is either stopped or deflected, more
or less, by almost every substance ; but all media
are to gravity perfectly transparent ; nothing is able
either to reflect, refract, or absorb it ; and two points
on opposite sides of the globe attract each other as
if there were absolutely nothing between them.

Again, gravitation, as Faraday has shown,[2] is at

---

[1] " Principles of Science," vol. ii., pp. 466, 467.

[2] *See* Faraday's paper on the " Conservation of Force," pp. 364,
366, 368, " Correlation and Conservation of Forces," edited by E.
L. Youmans, M. D.

odds with the fundamental doctrine of the conservation of energy, and also with that of inertia. The received idea of gravity as a simple attractive force between any two or all the particles or masses, at every sensible distance, with a strength varying inversely as the square of the distance, appears to Faraday to involve inconceivable inconsistencies. In the case of the diminution of the distance, say to one-tenth, and the consequent increase of the force a hundred-fold, it implies an actual *creation* of force, and that to an enormous extent; and in the reverse case, where the distance is increased tenfold and the power diminished to a hundredth of its previous amount, it implies an actual *annihilation* of force; effects requiring the intervention of Infinite Creative Power.

Again, the current idea of gravity supposes that a single isolated particle would have no gravitative force, but that, the moment another single particle (which by itself is also without gravitative force) is placed in relation to it, gravitative force springs up in both particles. This also implies the creation of force and the impossible consequences already referred to.

Again, if we consider the mutual gravitating action of one particle and of many, the particle A will attract the particle B at the distance of a mile with a certain degree of force; it will attract a particle C at the same distance of a mile with an equal power; if myriads of like particles be placed at

the given distance, A will attract each with equal
force ; and if other particles be accumulated around
it within the sphere, two miles in diameter, it will
attract them all with a force varying inversely with
the square of the distance. How are we to conceive of this force growing up in A to a million-
fold or more, and, if the surrounding particles be
then removed, of its diminution in an equal degree,
without admitting, according to the received definition of gravitation, the facile generation and annihilation of force ?

Or, if we take into consideration that property
of matter which is, perhaps, its most characteristic
property, that of inertia, we add still more to our
difficulty. When two particles of matter, at certain distances apart, attract each other and approach,
each, through that inertia, will store up a certain
amount of mechanical force, due to the force exerted. According to the doctrine of conservation, an
equivalent portion of the cause of attraction must
be thereby consumed ; and yet, according to the law
of gravity, the attractive force is not diminished,
but increased inversely to the square of the distance.
Conversely, if mechanical force from without be
used to separate the particles, this force is not stored
up by inertia, but disappears ; and, when bodies
have been moved to double the distance, the force
is only one-fourth as great.

If gravity is a property of matter, and possessed
of its inertia, these results are **truly inconceivable** ;

and if we regard it, as has been urged, as an immaterial principle, then either an equal inconceivability
is believed by Science, or Science grants the fundamental position of Religion—the existence and
credibility of the immaterial.

Or, take the undulatory theory of light—another
of the greatest triumphs of Science—and what mental stumbling-blocks present themselves! We are
asked to believe that the infinitely greater bulk of
matter in the universe is radically different from
that portion of it which comes under the observation of our senses, and makes up the globe we live
on ; we are asked, that is, to violate the scientific
principles of continuity, and of judging the unknown by the known. We are asked, again, to believe that all the molecular and interstellar spaces,
though they seem to be empty, are filled with a medium whose pressure, as before was noted, is calculated at seventeen billion pounds upon every
square inch. Though thus immensely more elastic
and solid than steel, it cannot be weighed nor seen,
and we move through it without the least pressure
from it. A gaseous medium, like air, strongly re-
sists the flight throught it of any swiftly-moving
body ; but the immense pressure of this medium has
apparently little or no retarding effect either upon
the larger bodies or the minute atoms constantly
moving in it. The most that has ever been attributed to it is a slight retardation of one or two of
those most feeble and unsubstantial of bodies, the

comets. But, if the ether behaves according to the universal laws of matter, it is impossible for bodies like the planets or the atoms to move themselves through its dense substance without the expenditure of force in pushing it aside, and, as an inevitable result, a continual decrease of all cosmical motion. But if, nevertheless, we imagine, as bold physicists have done, that the ether is exempt from this law, and suppose that it is frictionless—planets and atoms swinging in it without loss of motion—then we are involved in an equal difficulty ; for, as the ether takes no motion from the bodies moving in it, it consequently cannot impart nor transmit any motion to other bodies, and the whole use of the ether, and the necessity for supposing it as the medium for transmitting light and heat, disappears.

Such are the inconceivabilities and contradictions which we plunge into in the study of just two special points in scientific investigation. If we were to examine, in turn, the various departments of physical knowledge, we should find everywhere only similar results.

Leaving particular difficulties, let us, then, inquire into that which is the seat of all physical force, the subject of investigation in all departments of Science—matter itself in general. It is matter and its qualities, we are told, that explain every thing. What, then, is this " matter ? " We generally understand by it the common substance of all bodies. Bodies have many qualities; but the two qualities common to all bodies are volume and force. Considering the volume, or the extension of matter, the question arises, Is that divisible or indivisible? Down to the primary atom, it is universally conceded to be divisible; then comes a dilemma. If we say it is indivisible, that is something irreconcilable with its possessing volume or extent; for, however infinitesimally small, as long as it has any volume, it must have an under and an upper, a right or a left, side between which a division is conceivable. If the atom is not divisible, it cannot be extended, and hence cannot, by any aggregation of such unextended atoms, make an extended body. On the other hand, if we say, as Büchner does, that matter is divisible *ad infinitum*, then we can never arrive at what constitutes the reality of it; for, as long as a thing is divisible, it is a compound, and a compound has no reality except that of its component parts; and as no portion can be found, not composed of smaller parts, we shall never succeed in arriving at the ultimate element which alone can give reality to the aggregate. Moreover, as the process of division in search of the ultimate parts of matter has to be carried on beyond any finite limit, those ultimate parts must be less than any finite extension, and the former difficulty again occurs, How can they make up an extended aggregate?[1]

Again, if we consider the question of the con-

[1] *See* Janet's "Materialism of the Present Age," translated by Gustave Masson, p. 45.

tinuity of matter, we fall into similar dilemmas. If matter be continuous throughout all space, atom in contact with atom, then all differences of density, all expansion or compression, all motion, even, except such as that of Descartes's supposed vortices, is impossible. On the other hand, if matter be discontinuous, then we must either believe the inconceivability that matter can act where it is not, or we must suppose the force that passes through the void spaces of matter is not inseparable from matter: that is, we must grant the postulate of Religion—the existence and action of the immaterial.

Taking up, next, the other main element in the idea of matter, its force, and endeavoring to follow it out to its logical result, the scientific analyst finds another dead-wall to bruise his head. Is matter conceivably preëxistent to force, and really independent of it, though practically revealing itself only through it? So some seem to think. But just imagine matter separate from force, and what remains of it? Nothing but extension, as Janet[1] has well pointed out. How, then, is matter in itself distinguished from space? How can a portion of matter be discriminated from the portion of space corresponding to it? In no wise. Suppose, then, we take the other horn of the dilemma—say that force is the inherent quality of matter, not even in thought to be separated from it. The difference of a portion of matter from the space it occupies is

[1] "Materialism of the Present Day," p. 47.

now plain. It differs in its force. But as this is the only thing it differs in—as force is the only other factor besides extension always entering into it—is not this saying just what the opponents of materialism have always urged, namely, that matter really consists in simple force, located in space, and that the conception of a thing besides, called matter, was superfluous? "What do we know of an atom apart from its force?" is the pertinent question of Faraday. "You conceive a nucleus that may be called *a*, and you surround it with forces that may be called *m*. To my mind, your *a* or nucleus vanishes, and substance consists in the energy of *m*."

There are, it is true, perhaps the scientist will say, many things which we believe without yet understanding them, but we look forward to in time. But the mysteries of religion, involving as they do the notions of infinity and self-existence, are absolute mysteries, not merely now incomprehensible, but from our constitution as finite beings always to remain so. I do not care here to discuss this question of the knowability or conceivability of the Infinite. Were I to do so, I believe that it would be easy to show that this supposed difficulty is entirely due to certain common confusions of thought and ambiguities of language. That which is inconceivable, because of its contradiction to the laws of thought, is certainly unbelievable. But that which is inconceivable only by its overpassing the limits of our powers is not, therefore, to be thought non-

existent. That which is unpicturable to the imagination may yet be thinkable by the reason. That
which we cannot know in essence we may yet know
in its attributes and relations. That which we cannot know completely we may yet know not inadequately and not untruly. The infinitude of an object in quantitative respects does not make it unknowable in its qualitative attributes.[1] Spiritual
things are not graded by magnitude, but by perfection.

If we bear these distinctions in mind, we shall
not be troubled, I believe, by the alleged inconceivability of the infinite. But whether or not the
infinite is conceivable or knowable, the fact remains
—which I especially desire here to call attention
to—that science continually employs the conception
of the infinite, without hesitation, and builds with
it many of its proudest structures. In mathematical
calculations it is continually employed without distrust. In geometry and mechanics the idea of the

[1] A cylinder prolonged to infinity does not cease to be a cylinder
or become unknowable. Infinite space is still space, has the capacity of holding extended objects, and the same three dimensions—
length, breadth, and thickness. As Lewes justly says, laying it
down as an important formula: "The existence of an unknown
quantity does not necessarily disturb the accuracy of calculations
founded on the known functions of the quantity."

Thus, to give his illustration, although we may be unable to answer the question, "What is the value of $7x$ added to $5x$?" so
long as x remains without an assigned or assignable value, we are
absolutely certain that the result will be $12x$, *whatever* value x may
have.

infinite plays an indispensable *rôle*. The conceptions of the line, the circle, and the sphere, are inconceivable except through conceptions of the infinitely small. So in mechanics, the passage from
the axioms of uniform motion to other forms of
motion is made by the assumption of uniform motion through infinitesimal intervals. Astronomy
and geology, on the other hand, lead us to the cor-
relative infinitude, the infinitely large. As the telescope penetrates into space it brings to us inevitably
the question, "Is there a limit anywhere to space?"
That there should be a limit to space, a boundary
beyond which there should be no opportunity for
existence, is certainly unthinkable; but, if so, we
must accept the infinity of space with whatever in-
conceivableness properly belongs to it. As the geologist traces back the history of the world, he runs
athwart similar dilemmas attaching to time and
matter. It is unthinkable that time should have a
limit beyond which there would be no possibility of
duration or succession. But if not, then infinite
time, with its opposite inconceivability, must be accepted. It is inconceivable that matter should have
come into existence out of nothing. But the only
alternative is the equal inconceivability, that matter
has existed from all eternity. If theologians, with
their ideas of creation, are guilty of believing in the
first members of these pairs of inconceivables, those
who reject it must accept the second. In point of
fact they are quite generally accepted by the scien-

tific world. Mr. Proctor, in his lecture upon the
"Infinities around us,"[1] bears testimony to the acceptance by the astronomer of infinity of power,
infinity of space, and infinity of time in the universe. Especially do those who belong to the materialistic school, and find the ideas of theism inconceivable, make without scruple the most confident
affirmations of infinity. Strauss,[2] for example, declares that, "if we contemplate the universe as a
whole, there never has been a time when it did not
exist, ... the cosmos itself, the sum total of infinite worlds in all stages of growth and decay,
abode eternally unchanged, in the constancy of its
absolute energy, amid the everlasting revolution and
mutation of things." Vogt and Büchner[3] lay down,
as fundamental principles of their system, the eternity of matter and the immortality of force.

Prof. Haeckel, of Jena, whose book, "Generelle
Morphologie der Organismen," has been called "the
Bible of Darwinism," says of the theory of creation
(book ii., chapter vi., sec. 2): "The acceptation of
this is quite incompatible with one of the first and
chiefest of Nature's laws, one, indeed, universally
acknowledged—namely, with the great law that *all
matter is eternal.*"

Even Herbert Spencer falls into the same pit.
Though he has branded all ideas which involve infi-

[1] *Tribune Extra*, No. 15.
[2] "The Old Faith and the New," pp. 173, 174, American edition.
[3] *See* "Force and Matter," chapters ii. and iii,

nite self-existence as "pseudo-ideas," and consequently condemned all forms of theism, pantheism, and
materialism, as inevitably involving such inconceivabilities,[1] no sooner has he put theology, as he thinks,
hors de combat, and gone on to his positive scientific
construction, than he tells us that matter was both
uncreated and is indestructible, and that force always persists in unchanged quantity,[2] ideas necessarily involving infinite duration both in the past
and in the future. Yet if the infinite is an inconceivable thing, a pseudo-idea, a symbolic conception
of the illegitimate order, what saves these scientific
conceptions from vitiation by it? When the wariest
thinker is driven by continual dilemmas into accepting inconceivability either on one side or the other,
"why then," as Proctor asks, "dismiss the idea of
a God merely because he is beyond our powers
of conception?" The principle on which religion
reasons up to the infinite is not different from that
employed by the mathematician, the geometer, or
the astronomer, for the same purpose. It is, in fact,
the same, the peculiar and fundamental conception
of a limit, "the use of which," in proving the
propositions of the higher geometry, Whewell says,
"cannot be superseded by any combination of hypotheses and definitions."

"This principle of a limit," continues Whewell,
"leads to all the results which form the subject of

[1] "First Principles," Part I., chapters ii. and iv.
[2] Ibid., Part II., chapters iv. and vi.

the higher mathematics, whether proved by the consideration of evanescent triangles, by the processes of the differential calculus, or in any other way." In fact it is "when such processes as Newton deduced from the conception of a limit are represented by general algebraical symbols, instead of geometrical diagrams," that "we have then before us the method of fluxions, or the differential calculus, a method of treating mathematical problems justly considered as the principal weapon by which the splendid triumphs of modern mathematics have been achieved." [1]

The axiom which rules in all these processes is simply that "what is true up to a limit is true at that limit." Applying this to the limit of infinity, it gives us the rule that what is true throughout all finite grades, up to the infinite, is true at the infinite. What better vindication from science could theology desire for its constant claim that the qualities of justice, love, wisdom, and holiness, manifested throughout the finite and phenomenal scale, shining out the more clearly the higher the grade of being, must exist in the infinite reality above and behind the finite phenomena; and that, moreover, this infinite justice, love, and holiness, is not perhaps radically different from its finite manifestations, but, however immensely greater and more perfect, is essentially the same?

[1] Whewell's "History of Scientific Ideas," vol. i., pp. 152, 153.

CHAPTER VI.

SCIENTIFIC RESULTS.—THEIR UNCERTAINTY, INEXACT-
NESS, AND VARIABILITY.

THERE is still one other difference often insisted upon as justifying a difference in the comparative credit given to science and religion—the difference of results.

Though religion may perhaps use the same methods as science and aim at no more transcendental objects, yet, in practice, it is charged that she is never able to reach the exactness and the certainty for which science is distinguished. When science once puts her foot down, she never draws back. The received truths and forms of religion, on the other hand, are continually shifting. Its early phases were often gross and full of errors. Neither morality nor faith has any absolute standard, any unretreating course.

Again I answer, these are charges to which science as well as religion lies open. No difference exists here sufficient to justify contempt or disregard for religion on the part of scientific men, or those who accept current scientific doctrines and results.

No instance of sense observation is entirely exempt from the possibility of error or delusion. As has been already noticed, every sense has its limits, beyond which it fails either to discriminate or to perceive at all. Unusual conditions of observation cause mistakes in perception. Cross the fingers, and, while the eyes are shut, put a cherry between the sides usually separated, and two cherries, instead of one cherry, are felt. A torch whirled rapidly, or drops of water falling swiftly, seem to form a continuous line, the separate impressions running into each other. Without surveying the particular defects of all the senses, it will be sufficient to look at that sense which is most wonderful and perfect—vision. Its perfection is not absolute, but merely practical.

Prof. Helmholtz, in his lecture on "The Recent Progress of the Theory of Vision," gives a catalogue of some of the principal defects of the eye:

1. Chromatic aberration.

2. Spherical aberration and defective centring of the cornea and lens, together with the first defect, producing the imperfection known as astigmatism.

3. Irregular radiation around the images of illuminated points.

Helmholtz considers these defects so grave that he declares that "it is not too much to say that, if an optician wanted to sell me an instrument which had all these defects, I should think myself quite justified in blaming his carelessness in the strongest terms, and giving him back his instrument."

He then goes on to other faults :

4. Defective transparency.

5. Floating corpuscles (*muscæ volitantes*).

6. The blind spot, with other gaps in the field of vision.

But this is not all. " The inaccuracies and imperfections of the eye, as an optical instrument, and those which belong to the image on the retina, now appear insignificant in comparison with the incongruities which we have met with in the field of sensation. One might almost believe that Nature had here contradicted herself on purpose, in order to destroy any dream of a preëxisting harmony between the outer and the inner world. . . .

" In general, then, light, which consists of undulations of different wave-lengths, produces different impressions upon our eye, namely, those of different colors. But the number of lines which we can recognize is much smaller than that of the various possible combinations of rays with different wave-lengths which external objects can convey to our eyes. The retina cannot distinguish between the white which is produced by the union of scarlet and bluish-green light, and that which is composed of yellowish-green and violet, or of yellow and ultra-marine blue, or of red, green, and violet, or of all the colors of the spectrum united. All these combinations appear identically as white, and yet, from a physical point of view, they are very different."

Again, the eye cannot correctly estimate the comparative brightness of two luminous bodies which differ very much in brilliancy, for we know that the eye is constantly adjusting itself to the intensity of the light received, and thus admits more or less light according to circumstances. The moon, so bright at night, is pale and nearly imperceptible while the eye is yet affected by the vastly more powerful light of day. For this reason it is difficult to estimate any change in the form or comparative brightness of nebulæ, or of the zodiacal light. The appearance depends greatly on the varying darkness of the night and the keenness of sight of the observer, or the freshness or fatigue of the eye. In judging of colors, again, there is a difficulty arising from the fact that light of a given color tends to dull the sensibility of the eye for light of the same color.

No one has given a more compact catalogue of ways in which the senses are found insufficient than Lord Bacon in the "Novum Organum." "Things escape the senses," he says, "because the object is not sufficient in quantity to strike the senses, as all minute bodies; because the percussion of the body is too great to be endured by the senses, as the form of the sun, when looking directly at it in midday; because the time is not proportionate to actuate the sense, as the motion of a bullet in the air, or the quick, circular motions of a firebrand which are too fast, or the hour-hand of a common clock, which is too slow; from the distance of the object as to place, as the size of the celestial bodies, and the size and nature of all distant bodies; from prepossession by another object, as one powerful smell renders other smells in the same room imperceptible; from the interruption of opposing bodies, as the internal parts of animals; and because the object is unfit to make an impression upon the sense, as the air, or the invisible or untangible spirit which is included in every living body."

Moreover, besides these bodily hinderances to correct observation, there are the mental hinderances. Even when the utmost care is used in observing and recording, tendencies to error exist. Almost every observer has a bias that affects, more or less, his observations. The mind of man, as Bacon said, is an uneven mirror, and does not reflect the events of Nature without distortion.

Again, there may be circumstances connected with the object observed which may tend to distort it or cause us to observe it one-sidedly. There is always, for example, a prevailing fallacy, that our ancestors built more strongly than we do, arising from the fact that the more fragile structures have long since melted away. Prof. De Morgan has mentioned four ways in which one event may seem to follow, or be connected with another, without really being so.[1]

In consequence of these hinderances and pitfalls, the various sciences will lack more or less of the certainty commonly attributed to them. None have

[1] *See* " Essay on Probabilities," Cabinet Cyclopædia, p. 121.

done more to show this than the men of science themselves. Dr. W. B. Carpenter, speaking of the general belief that the scientific interpretation of Nature represents her not merely as she seems, but as she really is, says : "When, however, we carefully examine the foundation of that assurance, we find reason to distrust its security, for it can be shown to be no less true of the scientific conception of Nature than it is of the artistic or poetic that it is a representation framed by the mind itself out of the material supplied by the impressions which external objects make upon the senses, so that to each man of science Nature is what he individually believes her to be." Prof. Kingdon Clifford, in his lecture upon the " Aims and Instruments of Scientific Thought," delivered before the British Association at Brighton, 1872, discusses at considerable length the question, " What do we mean when we say that the uniformity of Nature is exact ? " and concludes that we mean by it " no more than this, that we are able to state general rules which are far more exact than direct experiment, and which apply to all cases that we are at present likely to come across."

Not only in general do scientific men admit the imperfections and inexactitude of science, but, in particular. Dr. Paget, in mentioning the advantages of the study of physiology, mentions as one of them, the fact that it is " a very uncertain and incomplete science," well adapted, therefore, he thinks, to disa-

8

buse young men of the too prevalent idea that a plain yes or no can be answered to every question that can be plainly asked, and that every thing thus answered is a settled thing, and to be maintained as a point of conscience. Herbert Spencer has recently shown, in his volume on the "Study of Sociology," the uncertainties that beset social science. The phenomena to be studied here, he states, are not of a directly perceptible kind, to be examined by scientific instruments, like those of astronomy or chemistry, nor are they to be recognized by introspection, like the phenomena of psychology. The disturbance of the various emotions and prejudices of the observers, the political, educational, patriotic, theological, and class biases, add to the difficulty. Thirdly, a danger still more subtile and difficult to escape from arises from the exceptional position of the observer, who is inevitably himself a part of the very aggregate that he studies, and cannot divest himself of the personal interests and partial predispositions arising therefrom.

In regard to political economy, what Daniel Webster said in 1830 is still, in great measure, applicable. "For my part," says Webster, "though I like investigation of political questions, I give up what is called the 'science of political economy.' There is no such science. There are no rules on the subject so fixed and invariable as that their aggregate constitutes a science. I believe I have recently run over twenty volumes, and from the whole, if I should pick out with one hand all the mere truisms, and with the other all the doubtful propositions, little would be left." Although since then we have had the able and laborious investigations of Mill, Bastiat, and Carey, nevertheless, I believe there is little more general agreement among political economists, and few more invariable rules that are unanimously accepted.

Even the most exact of sciences, astronomy, is far from perfectly exact. "Many persons," says Jevons,[1] "may be misled by the expression *exact science*, and may think that the knowledge acquired by scientific methods admits of our reaching absolutely true laws, exact to the last degree. . . . The very satisfactory degree of accuracy attained in the science of astronomy gives a certain plausibility to erroneous notions of this kind. . . . Kepler's laws are not proved, if by proof we mean certain demonstration of their exact truth. Even if we could observe the motions of a planet of a perfect globular shape, free from all perturbing or retarding forces, we could never perfectly prove that it moved in an ellipse. To prove the elliptical form we should have to measure infinitely small angles and infinitely small fractions of a second; we should have to perform impossibilities. . . . But, secondly, as a matter of fact, no planet does move in a perfect ellipse or manifest the truth of Kepler's laws exactly. . . . The mutual perturbations of the planets distort the

[1] Chapter xxi.

elliptical paths. Those laws, again, hold true only
of infinitely small planetary bodies, and, when two
great globes like the sun and Jupiter attract each
other, the law must be modified. . . . Even at the
present day discrepancies exist between the observed
dimensions of the planets' orbits and their theoretical
magnitudes, after making allowance for all disturbing
causes.[1] Nothing, in fact, is more certain in scientific
method than that approximate coincidence can alone
be expected. In the measurement of continuous
quantity, perfect correspondence must be purely ac-
cidental, and should give rise to suspicion rather than
to satisfaction." [2]

It is from measurement that the great certainty
of science, where it is certain, comes. " Obviously,"
says Herbert Spencer,[3] " it is this reduction of the
sensible phenomena it represents to relations of
magnitude which gives to any division of knowledge
its especially scientific character." As Davy said,
" Nothing tends so much to the advancement of
knowledge as the application of a new instrument."
But it is only the simpler things that are open to
even approximate measurement. After two centuries of labor the most eminent mathematical talent
has succeeded in calculating the mutual effect of
three bodies upon each other under the single force
of gravity *only approximatively.* Astronomers have

[1] *See* Lockyer's " Lessons in Elementary Astronomy."
[2] " Principles of Science," vol. ii., p. 73.
[3] " Recent Discussions," p. 162.

not even attempted the general problem of the simul-
taneous attractions of four, five, six, or more bodies,
resolving the general problem into so many different
problems of three bodies. But an atom of a single
substance, says Jevons,[1] "is probably a vastly more
complicated system than that of the planets and
their satellites. A compound atom perhaps may be
compared with a stellar system, each star a minor
system in itself. The smallest particle of solid
substance will consist of a vast number of such stellar systems, united in regular order, each bounded
by the other, communicating with it in some manner, yet wholly incomprehensible. . . . There is
every reason to believe that each constituent of a
chemical atom must go through an orbit in the mill-
ionth part of the twinkling of an eye, in which it
successively or simultaneously is under the influence
of many other constituents, or possibly comes into
collision with them. It is, I apprehend, no exag-
geration to say that mathematicians have scarcely a
notion of the way in which they could successfully
attack so difficult a problem of forces and motions.
Each of these particles is forever solving differential
equations, which, if written out in full, might perhaps belt the earth, as Sir John Herschel has beau-
tifully remarked."

In the simplest natural phenomena, therefore,
there will always be numberless factors whose exact
influence can never be ascertained. "Until we

[1] "Principles of Science," vol. ii., p. 453.

know thoroughly the nature of matter, and **the** forces which produce its motions," say Thomson and Tait,[1] "it will be utterly impossible to submit to mathematical reasoning the exact conditions of any physical question." The approximate solutions which are reached "are attained by a species of abstraction or rather limitation of the data, and thus the infinite series of forces really acting may be left out of consideration." In science, then, the problems solved do not reproduce the actual order in its real complexity, and the laws and explanations are more or less hypothetical, and apply to nothing which we see or feel. Even physical astronomy, where the nearest approximation to actual conditions is found, is full of assumptions and neglect of numberless discrepancies. It is assumed in it that the other millions of existing systems exert no perturbing influence on our system; that the planets are perfect ellipsoids with absolutely smooth surfaces and homogeneous interiors—assumptions, part of them, certainly untrue, as every hill and mountain show, and the rest very doubtful. In regard to other branches of science the same thing is true. Scientific investigators speak and calculate about homogeneous substances, perfect fluids and gases, inflexible bars, points at which the gravity of bodies is concentrated, uniform spheres, etc.; but in reality there are no such things in Nature. Take one of the simplest problems in mechanics, the use of a crowbar **to raise**

[1] "Natural Philosophy," vol. i., p. 337.

a heavy stone, and we shall find, as Thomson and Tait have pointed out, that we neglect far more than we observe.[1] If we suppose the bar to be quite rigid, the fulcrum and stone perfectly hard, and the points of contact real points, we might give the true relation of the forces. But, in reality, the bar will bend, the stone may yield a trifle, and the points of contact are not absolute points, and the extension and compression of the different parts involve us in difficulties which no mathematics can cope with. In a practical point of view, these effects are generally inappreciable; but, compared with absolute exactitude, there will always remain gaps not to be closed up.

Especially when we would know any of the higher orders of existence, there must be uncertainty in our knowledge. The inorganic is somewhat subjectible to measure, but, when we enter the realm of the vital or the mental, we come to that which can no longer be put into feet and inches, pounds and ounces. "We cannot," as Dr. W. O. Johnson recently warned his medical brethren, "describe the commonest chemical change going on in the body. We cannot define the simplest of the vital processes." In the words of the chemist Berthollet, "We know nothing of any one of them thoroughly, since a perfect knowledge of any one of them involves a perfect knowledge of all the laws and forces which continue to produce it." What shall we say,

---

[1] "Treatise on Natural Philosophy," vol. i., p. 337, etc.

then, of the higher problems of the intellectual and spiritual order? Here, Science finds herself in a realm of mystery. What measuring-rod can science put to the sense of beauty? By what weight-standard can it estimate the quantitative energy of a thought? By what calculus can right and wrong be reduced to foot-pounds? By what moral astronomy shall the track of free-will be predicted, and the infinite complications and ever-changing equilibrations of society be foretold?

"In human affairs, then," as Jevons well says,[1] "the real application of scientific method is out of the question."

Or take the measures with which science reaches its greatest precision—a precision oftentimes really marvelous. In comparison with these standards, the variability of conscience is pointed out, and the shiftings of moral judgment in different ages and peoples are declared to disprove the existence of any authoritative moral faculty, or at least to disprove the existence of any fixed standard of right and wrong. But is science really any better off in these respects? Has it any absolute standard measure, either of direction, time, weight, or extension, any more than religion of morality or faith? Not a bit. All the instruments with which scientific men perform their measurements are more or less faulty. A surface of mercury is supposed to be perfectly plane, but even in the breadth of five inches there is

[1] Vol. ii., p. 460.

a calculable divergence from a true plane of about
a ten-millionth part of an inch. A plumb-line is
assumed to be perfectly vertical, but, owing to the
attractions of mountains and other inequalities on
the earth's surface, this is never absolutely true, and
in extensive surveys has to be approximatively cor-
rected. In measuring time, the pendulum, admirable as it is, is not absolutely invariable. The
slightest change in the form or weight of the pendulum, such as changes of temperature, the slightest
corrosion of any part, or the most minute displace-
ment of the point of suspension, readily cause,
would falsify the result.

The best unit of time is the rotation of a freely-
moving body. But when we inquire where the
freely-moving body is, "no satisfactory answer,"
says Jevons, "can be given." Practically, the ro-
tating globe is sufficiently accurate, and no long
time has passed since astronomers thought it impossible to detect any inequality in its movement;
but it is now known that the friction of tidal
waves and the radiation of heat into space has
slightly decreased the rapidity of the earth's motion.
The moon's motion round the earth and the earth's
motion round the sun form the next best measure
of time. But these also are subject to disturbances from other planets or heavenly bodies, and
from the loss of energy through slight resistances
met in their passage through space. "We thus,"
says Jevons, "appear to be devoid of any hope

of establishing a sure standard of the efflux of time."

Turning to space measurements, we find it equally difficult to obtain any invariable standard.

To construct or preserve an unchangeable standard bar is something which is not possible, or at least cannot be shown to be possible. Passing over the practical difficulty of defining the ends of the standard length with sufficient accuracy, we have no means of proving that the substance of the bar does not contract or expand with age or temperature. It is certain that many rigid and invariable substances do change in dimensions both from age and temperature. If we take, as our unit, a certain fraction of the earth's circumference, this likewise is exposed to uncertainty from possible changes in the earth's magnitude and the difficulty of measuring the earth with sufficient accuracy. Or, lastly, if we take as a standard the length of a seconds pendulum, we must assume that the attraction of gravity at a given point, and the length of a sidereal day, remain entirely unchanged, neither assumption, as far as we can judge, being absolutely correct.

Similar difficulties beset attempts to obtain unchangeable weights or standards of density, mass, motion, or heat. Besides the disturbing conditions known, but impossible sufficiently to guard against, vitiating all these standards, there are also conditions which it is always possible may exist unsuspected.

The fact is, that the realm of experience, instead of being the favored seat of exact truth, can never give us any absolute certainty. In the words of Judge Stallo, at the conclusion of his remarkable articles on the "Primary Concepts of Science," [1] "there is no absolute system of coördinates in space to which the positions of bodies and their changes can be referred; and there is neither an absolute measure of quantity, nor an absolute standard of quality. There is *no physical constant.*" No absolute physical standard is even conceivable. The only absolute certainty is in the realm of ideas —of intuitions. As far as both science and religion are founded on them, they possess absolute certainty. As far as they are experimental, they partake more or less of the same relative validity and absolute uncertainty.

Whenever knowledge is destitute of absolute certainty, its history will represent a series of changes, whereby the absolute truth is more and more approximated. This is notably the case with religion. The rude phases which first it took on, the changes and transformations through which it has passed, have been common targets for comments by no means complimentary. But it is the same with science. Nothing is more contrary to the whole spirit of modern science, more absurd, indeed, to a modern intellect, than some of the scientific theories of Bacon. Kepler was full of chimerical notions, and we know from his own writ-

[1] *Popular Science Monthly*, December, 1873.

ings the numerous errors into which he fell. According to one of his earlier scientific works, the sun, stars, and planets, were typical of the Trinity, and God distributed the planets in space in accordance with the regular polyhedrons, etc. He gravely held that there could not be more than six planets because there were not more than five regular solids. His famous laws were the one true discovery among a score of vain and groundless speculations, and, even in the investigations that led him to these, he proceeded upon the false supposition that the sun's motion was requisite to keep up the motion of the planets, as well as to deflect and modify it. Even the acute genius of Huyghens did not prevent him from inferring that but one satellite could belong to Saturn, because, with those of Jupiter and the earth, it made up the perfect number of six. Before the time of Torricelli, physicists believed that Nature abhorred a vacuum, and this was the reason why water rose in a pump; but when Torricelli pointed out the fact that water would not rise more than thirty-three feet in a pump, nor mercury more than thirty inches, and thus above these points Nature had no objections to any vacuum, another cause had to be sought.

Van Helmont, who is immortalized by the study of the gases, believed that each part of the body had an archæus or special spiritual agent, subordinate to the principal archæus, which he located in the stomach, the seat also assigned by him to the intellect. The distinguished Vesalius, who, by his careful dissections, overthrew the hitherto unchallenged system of Galen, and first put anatomy upon a scientific foundation, did not dream of disputing that authority concerning the distribution of the blood, and therefore imagined that it distilled through the pores of the unbroken and impermeable portion, and steadily denied the existence of valves in the veins, although others had already observed them.

In modern times similar mistakes have been repeatedly made. The history of chemistry shows how substances have been confounded with one another. " Thus strontia," says Jevons,[1] " was never discriminated from baryta till Klaproth and Haüy detected differences between some of their properties. There is now no doubt that the recently-discovered substances, cæsium and rubidium, were long mistaken for potassium. The history of science is the history of the constant correction of earlier experimenters by later, causes of error which afterward are most apparent being at first overlooked. The Arabian astronomers determined the meridian by taking the middle point between the places of the sun when at equal altitudes on the same day. They neglected the fact that the sun' has its own motion among the stars in the intervening time. Newton thought that the mutual disturbances of most of the planets might be disregarded.

[1] " Principles," vol i., p. 273.

The expansion of quicksilver was long used as the measure of temperature, in ignorance of the fact that the rate of expansion increases with the temperature. Rumford, in his first experiment leading to a determination of the mechanical equivalent of heat, disregarded the heat absorbed by the box containing the water heated.[1] Lavoisier's ideas concerning the constitution of acids have received a complete refutation. He named oxygen the *acidgenerator* because he believed that all acids were compounds of oxygen, a generalization which further investigations disproved. Berzelius's theory of the dual formation of chemical compounds has met a similar fate. On its ruins has risen the New Chemistry. The simple splitting and pairing theory has been abandoned, and we are becoming familiar with the idea of unitary structure, molecular types, and transformations by substitutions and replacements, in which the arrangement of the elements is of as much consequence as the question which they are.

This succession of various theories is a phenomenon that cannot fail to strike him who studies the progress of scientific ideas as something common to all branches of physical investigation. In the early days of geology fossils were looked upon as the results of the fermentation of matter, or of terrestrial exhalations, or were supposed to be mere earthy concretions or sports of matter. When,

[1] Jevons, " Principles of Science," vol. ii., p. 86.

after two centuries of discussion, the belief that they were the remains of fossils gained sway, it was still held that the Noachian Deluge was the cause of all the past changes on the earth's surface. Discovery after discovery worked the refutation of this idea. Still all geologic changes were looked upon as sudden, of the nature of catastrophes: one school, the Plutonists, regarding fire as the great agent of all rock-formations; the other school, the Neptunists, holding that even the so-called igneous rocks were chemical precipitates from the waters. In the present century these theories have given way to the Uniformitarian theory, which refers the greatest geological changes to the agency of forces still in action, and this is now giving way to the Evolution theory. Recent discoveries, such as the finding of worked flints lying in strata, and in connection with extinct mammalia, hitherto supposed to be anterior to man; the discovery of the Eozoön in the Laurentian rocks of Canada; and especially the revelations made by the dredging expeditions, of the present contemporaneous formation of the chalk and lime deposits hitherto supposed to indicate different geologic epochs—have worked almost a revolution in geology. The strata of the earth's crust are hardly more various and irregular than the diverse theories in regard to their origin and history that from generation to generation have prevailed So in the history of biology. Passing by the mystical school, with its doctrines of sig-

natures and astrological fancies, as undeserving the
name of even primitive science, we have the Iatro-
chemical school of the seventeenth century, in which
the reactions of the acid and alkali, and various
other chemical principles and processes, explained
every thing; then, in the first half of the eighteenth century, the mechanical school of Borelli,
and the corpuscular hypothesis of Descartes, followed by the Vital Fluid theory, in which all the
peculiar functions of life are supposed to depend
upon a subtile ethereal substance diffused through
the organism, this again yielding to the two rival theories of modern physiology, the Psychical and the
Physical theories; one maintaining an immaterial
vital principle, the other that the processes of life
are but transformations of the various physical
forces.[1]

Electricity similarly was first spoken of as a
fluid, then as a force, now as an energy or motion
readily converted into thermal, molar, or molecular
motion of various kinds. To explain heat we have
had the phlogistic, the caloric, and now the molecular motion theory. For light, we have had the
Emission and the Undulatory theories; for the
heavens, the Ptolemaic and the Copernican systems; in regard to forces, the Cartesian and the
Newtonian conceptions. In the presence of the
new dynamics, the new botany, the new chemistry
of to-day, in the presence especially of those theo-

---

[1] Whewell's "History of Scientific Ideas," book ix, chap. ii.

ries most revolutionary to all scientific ideas—the natural selection and the evolution hypotheses—the natural philosopher of fifty years ago would feel that there was nothing for him to do but to learn his science over again, and learn it all differently. Great as have been the theologic changes in the last century, they are more than matched by the shiftings of scientific theory. If in former times the best men of science have made as many errors as it is now proved that they have, is it likely that the dicta of the present school of scientists are to remain forever unshaken? If the past errors, if the present possibility of error in some things, do not interfere, nevertheless, with the substantial trustworthiness and validity of present science, why should they with the trustworthiness and validity of religion?

CHAPTER VII.

POSITIVE SCIENTIFIC PROOFS OF RELIGION.

In the previous chapters I endeavored to show that, if the foundations of religion are insecure, those of science, also, for the same reasons and in the same way, are uncertain. Not only can this negative exposition be made, but positively it can be shown that religion has valid evidences similar to those of science. Physical investigation can claim no monopoly of scientific method; for, as Herbert Spencer says, it is nothing different from ordinary reasoning, but simply the processes of common-sense carried out with precision. Let us consider, then, the

SCIENTIFIC FOUNDATION OF RELIGION.

The starting-point of all science is in the observation of Nature. The various senses, sight, hearing, smell, touch, perceive various objects—star, rock, water, plant, animal; and notice their varied qualities, heat and cold, hardness, softness, perfumes, sounds, forms, etc. These are compared;

their likenesses and differences noted. Then classifications are formed—families, species, substances, forces, laws—and, as the result of these inductions, general propositions are laid down, the general principle ruling in this inductive process being to classify together the like things, separating them from the unlike, and to interpret the unknown by the known, not *vice versa.*

Now, the course of religious thought has been the same. It may not have been aware that it started with observation, and proceeded by induction, any more than M. Jourdain knew that he talked prose. It may even have claimed to reach its knowledge entirely through other sources. Nevertheless, like science, its work has been, for the most part, the interpretation of the facts of Nature, only it has taken them up with other aim, and pursued them in another direction. Mr. Huxley himself, urging upon clergymen the study of science, points this out. "The theories of religion," he says, "like all other theories, are professedly based upon matters of fact." [1]

If we examine even the rudest forms of religion, we shall find their genesis, as Mr. Tylor says, [2] in "the plain evidence of men's senses, as interpreted by a fairly consistent and rational primitive philosophy." Mr. Tylor has explained, at length, the various processes and reasonings which suggest

[1] "Lay Sermons," p. 60.
[2] "Primitive Culture," p. 387.

to the savage the doctrine of spiritual beings. To sum them up, they are as follows : Thinking men, at a low level of culture, observing the strange phenomena of sleep, trance, dreams, disease, death, are deeply impressed by them, and seek to account for them. What makes the difference between a live and a dead body—a conscious and an unconscious man ? What are these human shapes which appear in visions ? Looking at these marvelous facts, the ancient savage philosophers made the induction of what we may call an apparitional soul, or ghost-soul —an unsubstantial human image or shadow—the cause of life and thought, independently possessing the personal consciousness and volition of its corporeal owner, past or present, and able to leave the body and flash swiftly from place to place.

This conception of spiritual beings as the causes of life and motion once attained to, two great postulates of religion were natural inferences from it. As the soul or spiritual being was able to leave the body during life, and appeared in dreams after death, it was not involved in the destruction of the body at death, but continued to live on.

This was enough to establish for them the doctrine of the immortality of the soul. Then, as they looked upon the mighty marvels of earth and sky, so full of awe to primitive man, the grand conception of Divine Beings was reached.

The blazing sun which warmed and lighted **man ; the cloud which swallowed up the sun in the**

midst of its career, and shot its lightning-bolts upon
the earth ; the sea which now smiled so sweetly, and
now raved along the shore with tossing mane ; the
bubbling fount, the fruitful earth, the wind, the
mountain—here were powers which did not origi-
nate with man himself, over which he could exercise no control nor foresight, which were mightier
far than he. What is their nature ? Naturally he
applied to the explanation of the unknown outward
Nature the conception by which he had already explained his own life and movements. As he himself existed and executed his purposes and acted
upon the world through the spiritual being or soul
within him, so he believed that each celestial or
earthly body was itself or had as its mover an independent living spiritual being. Accordingly, he
offered to these spiritual beings worship, prayer,
gifts, sacrifices, rites, and ceremonies of various
kinds, such as he deemed would win their favor,
mollify their wrath, or persuade them to effect his
wishes.

In the widening experience of man, the rude
observations of early times have been made infinitely more full and exact. Further observation reveals
many errors in the primitive animistic theories of
human phenomena. Further observation shows Nature not to be ruled by numerous independent voli-
tions, but to be under the government of a single
uniform system of laws. The first crude theories
of religious interpreters must, therefore, be laid

aside. Theology has undergone many transformations between those early fancies and its modern forms. Nevertheless, its starting-point and its method to-day are the same, only carried out with more scientific rigor. Religion, with the help of science, whose aid is here invaluable, surveys the vast phenomena of the universe. It finds Nature not the same from all eternity, but ever changing. It finds these constant changes, however, directed by law. Every effect has some regular cause. Force is linked with force. Principle dovetails into principle. Creature is grouped with creature, forming an hierarchy of species, genus, order, and class. Thus the Kosmos discloses itself as a wonderful order. A luxuriant and exquisite loveliness beams thence upon the eye. Whether the devout or the undevout survey Nature, the beauty which graces it, ranging in scale all the way from the majestic glory of Alpine scenery to the symmetry of a snow-flake's facets, or the microscopic chasings of a diatom, cannot be unadmired. Again, in the admirable correlation of structure to environment, and of organ to function, in the mutual interdependence of animal and vegetable life, in the continuous self-adjustments of part to part and change to change, in the ingenious contrivances which minister to the prospective harmony of Nature, a marvelous exhibition of the adaptation of means to ends greets the glance of the observer. In every creature, tokens of providential impulses, stirring to activity, are revealed.

From the structureless germinal matter at the end
of a placental tuft which spontaneously burrows
into the surrounding pabulum to supply its want,
or the jelly-like amœba which pushes out portions
of the living substance and extemporizes with them
an organ to grasp its food, up to the insects which,
impelled by the needs of the coming generation,
build their rafts of eggs to hatch out after their
death, or the human infant seeking, untaught, the
mother's breast, all living things are impelled unconsciously to do what is needed for the maintenance
and preservation, not only of themselves, but of the
race. Through all changes and events a continual
progress from the more imperfect toward the more
perfect, a finer finish in Nature's handiwork, a
steady exaltation of faculty and power, a constant
increase in all that can minister to the well-being
or the happiness of living creatures, discloses itself. A work on natural theology is a treasury
of the most striking illustrations, out of the thousands that might be adduced, that witness to these
facts.

Then religion surveys the phenomena of human
nature. It finds there exalted powers and activi-
ties by virtue of which the impressions on the
senses, common to man with the brute, are given
with him a higher significance. It observes the
power of memory to retain and call up again the
past; the power of imagination to look forth into
the future, fly in thought to other climes, or build be-

fore the mind's eye ideal structures. It observes the faculties of judging and comparing, and the conceptions of likeness, number, time, and space, through which the facts of the world are classified and interpreted. It discovers intuitions, such as those of purpose, causation, and uniting law, by which the medley of events is reduced to an intelligible whole. It finds powers of abstraction and expression, by which man builds up the beautiful edifice of language and the solid masonries of logic. Unlike the bird or beast, man does not lie down in dull content. There is something in him that makes him dream of ideal excellence, fascinates him with every intimation of the infinite, draws him after the perfect. A divine disquietude fills him till he can realize them. The unalterable serenity which reigns elsewhere in Nature, in man gives place to the dramatic agitations of consciousness. For the rigid determinism, the iron fatality of the physical world, breaks off when we come to humanity, and another law appears—the law of freedom. Man finds that he enjoys the peculiar privilege of liberty of thought and liberty of will, that he has a power over Nature and over self, and that he can exercise it as he chooses. He labors, therefore, to make these conform to his wishes and conceptions, and minister to his delights. Knowledge of the world's order is in his hands only an instrument for acting upon it. He becomes, as it were, a second creator. He levels forests, he drains morasses, he tames and introduces this animal, he banishes that, he transforms the nature of plant and fruit. From brute matter he draws forth the skillful tool and the industrious, almost intelligent, machine, and multiplies infinitely his force. On the frescoed wall he fastens his glowing vision of beauty. In woven harmonies he/utters his unspeakable aspirations and infinite longings. In the forest-like arches of the cathedral he rears the enduring symbol of his reverence and awe for the divine. He looks upon the body of every fellow-man while living as animated by a being peculiarly sacred and vital; and, when the body is laid in the ground, it is his belief (in every race and nation, alike the most ignorant and the most cultivated upon the globe) that the *man* still lives on.

Most characteristic of all, there is in human nature a moral order more beautiful than any thing that art can show, more imperative in its inexorableness than any law of Nature—the order of duty. It is the high prerogative of man to perceive distinctions of right and wrong, unseen by any creature except himself, unseen by him through any organ of sense, revealed only to that marvelous inner eye —conscience. The right thus seen he feels bound to obey, though he has to go through fire and torture to do it. The wrong must be shunned, though the very heart-strings be torn asunder thereby. This moral law, as a French writer has well expressed it, "though it accord not with the selfish

9

ends of interest, the order of desire, nor the fickle trifling of his passing passions, nevertheless appears to him as the ideal end, the very crown of life, and he summons Nature to work with him for its realization."

Such are the phenomena which theology observes in Nature, without and within the circle of humanity.

The next step in the scientific method, as has been already noticed, is that of comparison and classification. To group together in the mind the things which are alike, and to distinguish them from the things unlike them, is, as Herbert Spencer states it, "not only the beginning of civilization, but the first step in the genesis of science."

Now, passing over all those minor classifications and those secondary causes which science studies so assiduously, minutely, and successfully, what ultimate classifications may be made and what first causes may be found by which to interpret the universe most fully and completely? This is just the question which theology has asked, and in its way answered. It has divided the universe into two great groups, each, within its own limits, containing the widest range of similar phenomena, and separated from each other by the broadest contrast of nature. One group contains all natural phenomena, such as weight, size, form, heat, color, motion; the other, all mental or spiritual phenomena, perception, reason, love, will, aspiration.

In the one group, inertia is the law; in the other, spontaneity. In the one, necessity; in the other, freedom. In the one, the phenomena have a definite relation to space—they have always a certain dimension, or local or extended movement; they can be weighed or measured. The phenomena of the other, on the contrary, exist in relation not to space, but to time; they have not extension, but duration; they cannot be either weighed or measured. The phenomena of the one are discerned by the senses; those of the other, by no sense, but only by consciousness itself. In the one group, every thing is divisible, even the smallest conceivable quantity is conceivably still further separable; in the other group, the subject affirms its indivisibility and identity. In the one group every thing belongs to the earthly and the finite. In the other group there is a constant attraction and rise toward that which lies higher.

These two great groups of phenomena having been thus clearly marked off from each other, religion then makes its inductions. As science infers, in explanation of the different phenomena exhibited by liquids and gases, that there is a different molecular structure as the respective substratum or subject of each; and in explanation of the diverse chemical properties of two chemical elements, such as potassium and oxygen, that there is a diverse atomic constitution as the subject of each; and again for the luminous vibrations still another subject, called ether, different from the subject of ponderable things—so religion, in explanation of the differences of material and spiritual phenomena, infers, as the subjects of each, distinct underlying realities, which it calls, in the one case, "matter," in the other, "spirit." This "spirit," it is true, has never been seen by mortal eye, probably never will be seen by mortal eye, and is therefore known only by a mental inference. But the same is true of molecule, atom, and ether. As these invisible things are inferred by science from the visible phenomena which it observes according to the mental law, that phenomena or qualities must belong to something as a subject, and that when the qualities are radically different the subjects must be supposed different, so is "spirit" the corresponding induction of religion from mental and moral phenomena.

As the imagination will not, in Tyndall's [1] language, "accept a vibrating multiple proportion, a numerical ratio in a state of oscillation," as the source of a train of ether-undulations, but "the scientific imagination, which is here authoritative, demands, as the origin and cause of a series of ether-waves, a particle of vibrating matter, quite as definite, though it may be excessively minute, as that which gives origin to a musical sound;" so, conversely, the religious imagination, in the religious realm equally authoritative, will not accept as the source of mental and moral states a vibrating

[1] "Fragments of Science," p. 135.

material particle, but demands, as the origin and cause of spiritual phenomena, a spiritual subject, quite as distinct from matter as its phenomena are distinct from material phenomena.

If an independent spiritual entity be a correct induction from spiritual phenomena, it will readily be seen to follow that this spiritual entity or soul, not being a compound, but an indivisible unit, as it constantly affirms, will not be dissolved by the dissolution of the body, but simply be released from its mortal coils. The same conclusion results also from the universal belief of mankind in a life after death. The philologists comparing the various languages of the Indo-European race—Sanscrit, Greek, Roman, Teutonic—find in them all certain common roots. They infer that these common roots must have been in use in the primitive Aryan race, before it left its ancient home in the table-lands of Asia and was dispersed in India, Greece, Italy, and Germany. From these common roots they tell us the social, political, and domestic conditions of our primitive ancestors. Again, geologists, observing the various appearances and peculiar illustrations of extreme antiquity which the earth presents, assume that they are not artificial or simulated, as bigoted defenders of the Mosaic record have sometimes contended, but that the testimony of primitive Nature may be relied upon as truthful. By parity of reasoning, religion infers from the universality of the belief in life after death that it is at once a primitive deliverance of human

nature, and as such ought to be accepted as vera-
cious.

The existence of the soul, now and hereafter—
this is the first great induction of religion. Then
follows the second, that of Deity. If we consider
the work of the palæontologist, philologist, geologist, or mechanician, we shall find them always
searching after the causes of things. What is the
origin of plants and animals? how did languages
begin? how did the earth come into existence and
into its present condition?—these are the questions
which are perseveringly studied by these physical
investigators. The principle upon which they proceed in their inquiries is, that all motion or change,
of whatever kind, had some ulterior cause. With
none of them is the business of scientific inquiry
closed with the first induction of a cause. Beyond
the proximate cause, they say, there must be a more
remote. No sooner is it found, for example, that
the peculiar scratches on rocks and upon banks of
characteristically-shaped stone, running across the
mouth of certain valleys in Scotland, are caused by
ancient glaciers, than the inquiry is made, "What is
the cause of these glaciers?" If they are recognized
as products of snow long and tightly pressed together, then the snow must be traced to its cause in
the action of extreme cold upon the moisture of the
air; and now a cause must be sought for this excessive cold which no longer exists in the same regions.
If this again be plausibly referred to a change in the

earth's orbit, its distance from the sun diminishing the amount of heat received by the earth, the investigator does not cease his inquiries, but demands an explanation of this change of orbit. And when this is found in a secular change in the direction of the earth's axis, still traceable, the torch of inquiry is brought to bear upon the very origin of the planetary system.

Thus the man of science is led farther and farther back, each secondary cause of the chain resolving itself as soon as reached into an effect of something else. This chain may run on to more and more remoteness. It may reach greater and greater simplicity and power. Nevertheless, the mind cannot find any satisfactory resting-place at any point of it, nor can it be satisfied to pursue indefinitely this phenomenal series. It conceives necessarily a first cause, a commencement, not merely for each part, but for the whole of the chain—an ultimate cause dependent upon nothing previous. It is the value of every true step made in philosophy, Newton said, that it brings us nearer to this first cause. " The business of natural philosophy" —these also are the words of the greatest of scientific authorities—" is to deduce causes from effects till we come to the very first cause, which certainly is not mechanical."

Now, it is just this path and end that religion pursues. It is true that of late men of science have themselves held back from taking the last step, to the Ultimate Source, as a thing beyond their proper province. But they ought not to object to religion's doing it in strict accordance with the method of science up to the point where the province of the latter was thought to cease. Some such ultimate source or first cause must be conceived. For the universe is not an eternal quiescence. It is in constant change, constant motion. And these changes and motions are part of a series actually existing and progressing. No matter what intermediate causes or agencies there may have been, the mind is not satisfied to stop with any of these, but passes farther and farther back, seeking the first cause, which must some time have first started the series. Now, this first cause cannot be matter itself; for matter has no spontaneity of action. The essential idea of matter—an idea which is fundamental to all scientific dealing with it—is that matter is inert; remains in its present condition forever, unless disturbed by some external agency. If matter did not observe this law, no science of it would be possible. In whatever condition and position matter originally existed, in that it must always have remained. To start the evolution of the universe, some external agency, possessed of spontaneity, must be inferred. As the only spontaneous agent we know of is free-will, the will of some Supreme Being must be regarded as the great First Cause.

A similar induction results from examining the nature of the proximate causes of change. A light-

ning-flash, for example, was found by Franklin,
in his famous experiment with the kite, to be of
the same nature as an electric discharge. The electric discharge was attributed to the action of electric fluid, but further investigation showed it to
be a case of molecular motion. Heat, light, sound,
have all likewise, in turn, been found to be modes
of motion, capable of conversion one into the other.
Going one step farther back, all motion is found
to have its source in some force—gravitative, cohesive, repulsive, chemical, or other kind. As
Herbert Spencer says, "We come down finally
to force as the ultimate." What, then, is this
last universal cause, this wondrous force? We do
not actually observe force in the external world at
all. When we observe a change in the external
world, all that is really observed is the following of
one event by another. We believe that there is
force working this succession, because when the line
strikes us we feel force, and especially because in
acts of the will we are conscious that we exert force.
" Undoubtedly," says Mr. Huxley,[1] " active force is
inconceivable except as a state of consciousness, . . .
except as something comparable to volition." Sir
John Herschel similarly says,[2] " In the only case in
which we are admitted to any personal knowledge
of the origin of force, we find it connected, pos-

[1] Article entitled " Bishop Berkeley on the Metaphysics of Sensation," *Macmillan's Magazine*, 1871.
[2] " Familiar Lectures," p. 461.

sibly by intermediate links untraceable by our **faculties**, but yet indisputably *connected* with volition,
and by inevitable consequence with *motive*, with
intellect, and with all those attributes of mind in
which—and not in the possession of arms, legs,
brains, and viscera—personality consists." To these
names I might add the names of Carpenter, Spencer, Grove, and Wallace, in science—not to speak
of eminent authorities in philosophy, all of whom
derive our knowledge of force from our volitional
and mental experiences. As in the only case where
we know force directly we find it to be an attribute
of will and intelligence, an energy and expression
of spirit, we must infer next, in accordance with the
steps already taken, in accordance with the general
rule of science, to interpret the unknown by the
known, that force everywhere else is but an energy
and expression of spirit—and of what other spirit
can it be than of the One Infinite and Almighty
Personality whom we call God?

Drawing another inductive line, religion reaches
the same conclusion. From the wise adaptation of
means to ends in vegetable and animal life, the
physiologist and anatomist are accustomed to infer
certain designs or purposes as their explanation, and
they freely employ this idea of design to assist them
in solving the problems of their departments. Dr.
Paget,[1] speaking of the study of physiology, claims
as one of its advantages that it " is a science of de-

---

[1] Youmans's " Culture demanded by Modern Life," p. 139.

signs and final causes. . . . In the inorganic world," he says, " we seem to come nearer to the efficient than to the final cause of events. But in the organic world the reverse is true ; purpose, design, and mutual fitness, are manifest wherever we can discern the structure or the actions of a part ; utility and mutual dependence are implied in all the language and sought in all the studies of physiology. The efficient causes and the general laws of the vital actions may be hidden from the keenest search ; but their final causes are often nearly certain."

In the history of physiology, Whewell has shown that those who studied the structure of animals were irresistibly led to the conviction that the parts of this structure have each its end or purpose ; that each member' or organ not merely produces a certain effect, or answers to a certain use, but is so framed as to impress us with the persuasion that it was constructed *for* that use. This persuasion directed the researches of Harvey. By the assiduous application of this principle, as he himself constantly declared, Cuvier was enabled to make the discoveries that have rendered his name so illustrious ; and it has been dwelt upon as a favorite contemplation, and followed as the most certain of guides, by the best anatomists and biologists. Moreover, from such cases of curious adaptation, science has not alone affirmed design, but also some Designer. One of the most astonishing of modern discoveries is that of the extreme antiquity of man, antedating, probably, the date formerly assigned by tens of thousands of years. How is it that science has been able to establish this? Simply by the discovery, in certain positions, of articles which it inferred were of human workmanship—bits of pottery under fifty feet of Nile-mud; instruments of bone or stone under thirty or forty feet of peat; flint axes, spear-heads, daggers, and knives, sometimes rudely carved with the representation of an ibex-head, a reindeer, or a rhinoceros, found in the drift of the Tertiary period in connection with the bones of extinct animals, such as the mammoth, cave-bear, or woolly rhinoceros. And why was it judged that these articles were of human origin, rather than natural? Only through the principle, either expressly stated or clearly implied, that instruments, fashioned in accordance with a regular plan, and adapted to an intelligent purpose, could not be the result of chance, or of unintelligent force or unconscious principles of order, but must have had intelligent—that is, in this case, *human*—makers.

In the same way—employing the same principles of reasoning—religion argues, from the evidences of fitness and contrivance in the world, intelligent design, and from the intelligent design an Intelligent Designer of supreme power and wisdom, equal to the supreme work manifested in the universe of creation. The theological argument is of the same kind as the reasoning of the archæologist,

only vastly more cogent in proportion as the instances of adaptation from which the theologian
starts are incalculably more numerous and curious
than those of the physical inquirer. The proofs
of design which the theist reasons from are not
drawn from a few scratches on a bone, or a hole
drilled through a piece of obsidian, or a few sharp-
ened bits of flint, now and then found in a gravel-
pit or a cave. They are present wherever we turn
our eye: in the coincident mathematics of plant
and planet; in the untaught geometry of the bee-
hive; in the admirable correlation of lung and air,
sound and hearing, light and sight; in the mutual
ministries of male and female, life and death, matter and spirit. From the wayside seed, laden with
future provision for the folded germ, to the clus-
tered systems, swinging in noiseless motion and
perfect poise through the ethereal spaces, all Nature testifies to the Arranging Mind that has marshaled the atomic armies according to well-ordered
plan.

It is true that scientific men, of late, have ob-
jected strongly to religion's employment of the
teleological argument. They charge that it leaves
the field of experience to launch into that of unverifiable conjecture. If so, they but condemn their
own practice in the field of anatomy, archæology,
and physiology.

If no man of science will accept a poniard fashioned from a reindeer's horn, or the rude repre-

sentation of the reindeer carved on its handle, as having come into existence by some chance combination of matter, or blind working of natural force, without the aid of designing mind, will he maintain, will any one maintain, that such chance combination of matter, or blind working of natural force, could bring into existence the *breathing man* that carved it and the *living* reindeer thus depicted? It is represented that, by showing how certain effects necessarily follow from certain antecedent conditions, all ground for supposing a prospective purpose is removed. "Because the fish," we are told, "has fins and gills, therefore, it uses them, and swims in the water. That is all. There is no need to suppose the fins and gills were made for that use." But how does the first truth militate against the last? If a purpose is wisely carried out, the means employed will always be such as lead naturally and necessarily to the end aimed at. To show that there is no design in the case, it ought to be shown, not that the structure of the fish naturally results in his swimming in the water, but that it is opposed to it. Nor do the theories of natural selection and evolution, if we suppose them already established, give any such fatal blow to the teleological argument as it is urged that they do. The inference of design is not to be removed by showing that the present form or adaptation is not the original one, but a development from some rude structure, a modification of some more primitive function, and that the

line of proximate causes and evolving conditions
can be traced back to a remote past and a very different natural condition, even perhaps to some primeval nebula of glowing gas. All this but shifts
the point of action and method of work of the designing intelligence, but does not diminish or abolish
the necessity of inferring it. On the contrary, it
increases the measure of Creative Mind to be supposed. For in that glowing gas were cradled all
the elements of the earth-to-be. The special adapta-
tions that now have been evolved lay latent there,
and were necessarily unfolded from the general order. But whence that general order—that orginal
tuning of force to law, and matter to harmonious
rhythm, and that exquisite adjustment of the whole
vast net-work of kosmic tendencies, so that Nature
should build itself up in beauty, and the strong ever
come forth from the weak, and the better proceed
always from the good, in an undeviating progress,
till the ascent is made from crystal and plant up to
the reasoning man ?

Here is a greater need of intelligence than ever.
Unless Nature be endowed with intelligence, there
is no reason that we know why it might not have
remained a perpetual chaos—a chronic anarchy of
discordant elements, incapable of stable organization.
Certainly the original arrangement and constitution
of matter might have had any one of a million various positions and properties, and each in the process
of evolution would have given a different result.

To choose out of the infinite variety of possible primitive arrangements, with their corresponding various results, just that one first arrangement and particular rudimental structure that in gradual, necessary unfolding would work out just the present admirable result, is a thing requiring fore-thinking wisdom far more than any instantaneous creation. " Natural evolution," says Prof. Owen, " by means of slow physical and organic operations, through long ages, is not the less clearly recognizable as the act of an adaptive mind because we have abandoned the old error of supposing it to be the result of a primary, direct, and sudden act of creational construction."

Even a Darwin, describing the wonderful contrivances existing in some of the orchids, by which their fertilization by insect go-betweens is secured, is compelled in spite of himself to resort to the language of design to express the facts; and Moleschott, the chief of the German materialist school, in an introductory address delivered at Turin, while fore-warning the investigator against guessing at final causes, yet would not have it believed that he is " rash enough or blind enough to refuse to Nature a design and an end. All those whose ideas I share by no means deny the *telos* which they guess, which they even sometimes perceive in Nature."

Again, from the spiritual wants of human nature, the inductive line leads to the same conclusion. One of the constant assumptions of scientific investigators is that a constant harmony exists between the structure and the environment of any living thing. "Wherever there is a constitutional want," the *savant* says, "there is a corresponding provision for meeting it." If he finds portions of the fossilized remains of a hitherto unknown animal, and by it recognizes its digestive apparatus as adapted to flesh food, then he knows that it must have had claws and jaws suitable for rending its prey ; if he finds its digestive organs ruminant, then he is assured that the animal had teeth for cropping grass, and that there was grass or other vegetation for it to crop. If he finds, as was found by the late Atlantic dredging expedition, animals at immense depths in the sea possessed of good eyes, he makes the induction that there is also there vegetable food for the animals to live on (though none was actually found), and light for the eyes to see by (though ordinary sunlight, according to his calculations, could not penetrate these depths). If he is an evolutionist, like Herbert Spencer, whenever, in tracing down the line of descent he comes to a new species or a modification of an old one, there, he supposes, some new combination of external conditions took place corresponding to the inward change. Even for life itself he can find no better definition than "the continuous adjustment of internal relations to external relations."

By the same logical principle, religion draws, from our felt need of the Divine to realize our ideal aspirations, from our inability to remain satisfied, as other creatures are, with the fleshly and the earthly, the induction of a Being corresponding to these demands of human nature. The inward want, rooted in our deepest nature, of a Personal Object to whom to direct our love, our worship, and our instinctive prayers—a Heavenly Model to serve as the guide and inspiration of our perfecting, an ever-present Friend whom we may seek in all sorrow and trouble —this inward want implies, somewhere outside of us, the Infinite Power and Absolute Perfection which alone maintains human nature in that harmonious adjustment with its environment which is found everywhere else in the world.

Once more, when the scientific explorer, unearthing the antiquities of Egypt or Assyria, discovers some tablet inscribed with laws, he not only infers that some one carved the sentences upon the stone, but also that they came from the mind and heart of some one—king, minister, or counselor. And, if the law be wise and just, its author is believed to have been wise and just. If, by further researches, other acts of this king or minister are discovered, and they are uniformly found to be such as would promote the happiness of the people, and would carry the nation constantly forward to higher and higher stages of physical, intellectual, and moral improvement, the historian does not hesitate to assign to him the attribute of benevolence.

Similarly, religion proceeds from the observation of the moral law to the induction of a moral Lawgiver. The profound sense of personal obligation to do the right and avoid the wrong, testifies, the theologian claims, to a Holy Ruler. Unless these most imperative convictions, these highest distinctions of human nature, are idle dreams, they must be the edicts of a righteous Governor. And the profuse beauty, the constant progress exhibited in this Ruler's works, especially the abundant means of happiness provided for all creatures, compel us to recognize goodness and love as among his most distinguishing qualities.

Finally, religion takes the last step of the scientific method by applying to these great inductions the test of verification.

To the hesitating novice and the flaw-picking doubter, Religion's common injunction is, "Just try my teachings, and see for yourself if they do not authenticate themselves." And, whenever the trial is fairly made, the further harmony between the inductions of religion and the experience of human life is triumphantly shown.

One of the most conclusive tests of science is that of concomitant variations. John Stuart Mill, in his system of logic, makes it the fifth canon of induction. When Faraday showed that, by making or breaking or reversing the current of the electromagnet, he had complete control over a ray of light, this was held to have proved the relation of cause and effect between magnetism and light. Let a man, then, make the experiment of dealing with

himself and his fellows on two opposite supposi-
tions. Let him, for a first experiment, regard and
treat men as soulless animals. How poor, how out
of joint, then, are all the results he meets with!
Why is it, if this view be true, that he cannot
reach his loftiest and most delicate development
on any such theory? Why is it that men so fool-
ishly sacrifice the most useful to the ideal—the
most needed bodily comforts and the most brilliant earthly advantages to a worthless spiritual
improvement? Why is it that even life itself is
sacrificed that this chimera of a soul may receive no
stain?

But if a man, on the contrary, will live as if
he had a soul and as if his fellow-men likewise had
souls, each day will bring him confirmation of the
great truth. In its light there are made plain to him
the puzzles which before were so incomprehensible—
this mystic attraction toward the Infinite and the
ideal, this discontent with our highest attainments,
this remorse for the smallest transgressions, this
strange fact in the realm of mind (the one exception
in the animated kingdom), that even the most fully
developed should not begin to reach a typical perfection. He comprehends now why it is that all human
glory and happiness and possession are so transitory,
and yet how the human heart with immortal fidel-
ity and hope can tell the grave that it claims in vain
aught beyond the mouldering robe of him whom it
loved.

The continued growth of thought and affection, even until the very last, though the body long ago passed its meridian and commenced its decline; the curious powers of the mind, seemingly independent of the senses, such as are exhibited in somnambulism, trance, clairvoyance, and similar phenomena; the utter inability of the subtlest science to find any adequate material or physical explanation of consciousness and the conscious powers—each affords renewed verification to the religious postulate, "Man is the possessor of a spirit."

So, too, when a man lives as if there were no God, he experiences the confutation of his atheism in his daily stumbles over the divine laws. But when a man honestly makes the experiment of acting steadily as if in the presence of a heavenly Father, he finds corroborative witnesses in every day's events. In whatever place he bows in sincere worship to this Adorable Being, he finds it good to be there. As often as in sincere prayer he seeks, from above, light in the perplexities of duty, or help in the hard battle of life, he receives the blessed answer—a heavenly beam upon his way, a God-given strength in the dusty conflict. Whenever, at bitter cost to his own desires and pleasures, he has yet obeyed the higher law of the Holy One, he has heard in his heart the approving whisper of a Divine voice. Whatever may be urged against the power of prayer to modify external Nature, the spiritual inward efficiency, the blessed reality of Divine communion, is known by the direct experience of millions.

In the fortunes of kings and private citizens, in the rise and fall of states, in the fluctuations of races and the vicissitudes of society, in every case of conduct, there is shown, to use Matthew Arnold's favorite phrase, "an Enduring Power, not ourselves, which makes for righteousness." Reward and retribution this Power allots in strict conformity to obedience or disobedience of the Divine Commandment. Every student of history knows how strange oftentimes are these vindications of God's moral law. How curiously innocence is justified, evil unearthed! The engineer of vice hoist with his own petard, Haman hanged on his own gallows! How sublime are the verifications of an Almighty Friend which the records of the past, the fresh life of the present, afford! Witness the strength which the weakest, trusting in him, have drawn to bear superhuman burdens; the bursting of the rockiest heart, under the heavenly touch, into sweet blossoms of tenderness and charity! Behold the sereneness with which pain and anguish can be borne, the bright faith with which the mourner can stand by the fresh-filled grave, the courage with which the champion of the right faces poverty, odium, perpetual annoyance, nay, goes to the stake or the gallows, assured of his vindication, hereafter on earth and at once above. Whatever contradictions, anomalies, enigmas, the infinitely-varied phenomena of life can present to religion, the sacred Œdipus, by one or the other of her two great truths, the existence of the soul and the existence of God, can always present a solution.

What Whewell calls the consilience of inductions—the leaping together of numerous facts of different kinds from unconnected quarters to one point, every new discovery or hitherto troublesome exception taking at once a position in harmony—is here wonderfully exemplified. It is a characteristic of the theistic argument. In the exposition which we gave of the theistic induction, it will be remembered how line after line of inference converged to the same point; and here, in the process of verification, we see the same thing afresh.

"Now," as Whewell says,[1] "that rules springing from remote and unconnected quarters should thus leap to the same point, can only arise from *that* being the point where truth resides. Accordingly, the cases in which inductions from classes of facts altogether different have thus *jumped together* belong only to the best-established theories which the history of science contains." For examples in which it has been especially exemplified, Whewell refers to the "Theory of Universal Gravitation" and the "Undulatory Theory of Light," and says that the Consilience of Inductions in them is considered as establishing them beyond all doubt. "No example can be pointed out in the whole history of

[1] "Novum Organum Renovatum," p. 88.

science, so far as I am aware," adds Whewell, "in which this Consilience of Inductions has given testimony in favor of an hypothesis afterward discovered to be false."

Stronger verification, then, than this would hardly seem to be desired of religion by any one. Yet, if it is demanded, it has a further confirmation—that of prediction. "There is no more convincing proof," says Prof. Jevons, "of the soundness of scientific knowledge than that it thus confers the gift of foresight." "Prevision," says Auguste Comte, "is the test of true theory." The astronomer's predictions of the movements of the planets, the occurrence of eclipses, the return of comets— even, as in Leverrier's discovery of Neptune, the existence and movement of a hitherto unknown body—afford the most conspicuous proof of the correctness of the Copernican system and the Newtonian laws. Even so have the prophets of old and the seers of God, in all time, through their comprehension of the great laws of moral gravitation, been able to foretell the course of states and the coming eclipses of individual and national glory. They have reckoned beforehand, according to the calculus of Divine Sovereignty, the setting of unholy stars, now proudly flaming in the zenith, and the triumphant rise of unsullied orbs, veiled then, though they were, in darkness—and, lo! it has come to pass even as they have said. If all supernatural instruction or illumination be denied to the prophetic voices of ancient and modern times, then the amazing power of insight, which must be ascribed to normal spiritual vision, as developed by religion, testifies with equal significance to the truth of the great principles on which religion is based.

Thus has religion positive foundations of the same kind as science, and they may be built up in a genuine scientific order. Doubtless a sharp scientific critic would find objections to such an inductive demonstration of religion. He would charge that these so-called inductions were not complete and exact, but imperfect—at best, only approximated perfection. He would say, "They are not simple colligations of facts, but they are theories built up and superimposed upon them. They are not cautious, exhaustive generalizations of coexistences; but they are hypotheses to which you have boldly leaped. And the verification you appeal to, though in much seeming to be given, is also in much wanting."

Now, these objections I should not altogether deny; but I should give to them this twofold answer, which ought fairly, it seems to me, to stop the mouth of the scientific objector, or of any objector who usually accepts, without hesitation, current scientific conclusions: First, in the previous chapters it has been shown in general that every one of these objections applies to science as well as to religion. Secondly, in the positive presentation, in the present chapter, not a single medium of proof is employed in regard to which it is not or cannot be shown that the very same argument, or its counterpart, is customarily and confidently employed by science. If one is to be rejected, then both should be rejected; if one is to be trusted, then both should be trusted.

To sum up, then, the argument of the last four chapters. Science, equally with religion, has a faith-basis. It uses intuition, authority, evidence, and probable inference, and is often destitute of possible verification. Science, no more than religion, can withhold nor does withhold its belief from the supersensual, the immaterial, or the inconceivable. Inexactness, uncertainty, and variation in the results of its labors, are faults found in science as well as in religion. On the other hand, religion, as well as science, has an experimental basis. It grounds itself on observation; it proceeds by induction, and it confirms its truths by verifications and previsions.

In this similarity of science and religion is there not something that should have practical influence with that daily-increasing number who, while accepting implicitly all the established truths and even the wildest speculations of science, look upon religion with suspicion, if not contempt? We commend to all such the words of Huxley: "By science I understand all knowledge which rests upon evidence and reasoning of a like character to that which claims our assent to ordinary scientific propositions, and if any one is able to make good the assertion that his theology rests upon valid evidence and sound reasoning, then it appears to me that such theology must take its place as a part of science."

I respectfully ask why the fundamental truths of religion do not already stand in that category with as good a right as the greater portion of what is called science?

CHAPTER VIII.

CONCLUSION.

A survey, then, of the relations of Physical and Religious Knowledge will bring a candid inquirer, I believe, to these conclusions: There is no necessary and rightful antagonism between Science and Religion. The actual opposition existing is due to the fact that each is, in many things, ignorant of itself and ignorant of the other. A fuller mutual acquaintance will so disclose to each its respective field that former intrusions shall cease, and will so fix the identity of each that other enemies shall not, as hitherto, be mistaken for it. More thorough knowledge will also show that the claims both have made to exclusive knowledge and supremacy cannot be sustained. Each has similar weaknesses; each has similar supports. Neither can overthrow the other with safety to itself. Each, in fact, needs the other, and should make of it an ally.

Without Science to correct and guide it, Religion is constantly going astray. The countless excesses and irrationalities of superstition, the varied corruptions of every faith, adoration of stick and

stone, lizard or bull; devil-worship, witchcraft, orgies of Bacchus, devouring rites of Moloch, and
unclean sacrifices to Venus—all these illustrate the
mournful aberrations into which devotion inevitably runs when divorced from understanding. Zeal,
without knowledge, as surely curses the world as
with knowledge it blesses it. Religion should en-
courage and urge the study of science, rather than
forbid it. The Church, instead of anathematizing
the great interpreters of Nature, should canonize
them. The truly devout behold God's footsteps
everywhere; and everywhere, in the depths of the
earth as in the heights of the sky, in forms of
matter as in the thoughts of men, should search for
" the fullness of him that filleth all in all."

The whole universe is the embodiment and manifestation of its Creator. Every ray that streams
from every star, every leaf that hangs on every tree,
each living structure, each moving creature, tells the
attentive student something of the thoughts and
character of the Divine Artist. Nature, then, to
the religious man, is God's oldest Testament, his
most direct Scripture. The ideas disclosed in it are
God's thoughts; Natural laws, Divine laws; Natural History, a chapter of Natural Theology. To
every new investigation of the physicist, Religion
should say God-speed; to every new discovery of the
savant, All-hail. The finding of a *Codex Sinaiticus*
should not rejoice the Church more than the discovery of a new law in Nature.

And Religion needs not only to accept the corrections and recognize the coadjutorship of Science in disclosing the ways of God, but it should engraft into itself, I believe, more of the scientific spirit. Instead of aiming to defend systems already established and to bolster up foregone conclusions, it should go simply with inquiring mind to the eternal facts. Casting aside all theological prepossessions and pride of opinion, it should interrogate carefully all the oracles of the world, without and within, and patiently await, and humbly receive their answers. Its only test of conclusions should be their truth or falsehood—not their supposed soundness or unsoundness, their flatteringness or humblingness, their pleasure or their pain. It should never feign certitude when it possesses none. It should discriminate to itself, and own in its public teaching the difference between what in its realm is known and what is but guessed at. It should employ more constantly the scientific methods, gleaning its evidence from as wide a field as possible; sifting it with care, retaining only what is fact, verifying each theory in some satisfactory way before accepting it as proved.

Theology, as I have endeavored to show, is fully able to bear such a scientific ordeal. In its essentials, if not in other respects, it has all the elements of an inductive science. "It includes," as has truly been said, "a multitude of positive facts—facts of observation and experience having a relationship with each other, and hence capable of classification and generalization, giving us positive knowledge up to a certain point, and beyond that it includes a domain of truth involved in the facts observed, and to be divined by laying under those observed facts general conceptions or hypotheses, which, though larger than our experience, must yet be true to our experience." Thus Religion is capable of being made a genuine Science, and it will never, I believe, maintain the purity, attain the stability and accuracy, reach unto the depth and breadth of truth which is within the demands of its grand mission unto mankind, until it thus weds Science to itself.

And, similarly, Science needs the help and inspiration of Religion to fulfill the true measure of its usefulness. Religion, without Science, is like writing a history without facts; Science, without Religion, is a biography without a subject. Religion, without Science, is a pyramid without base; Science, without Religion, is the pyramid without apex.

No one can earnestly study Nature without taking the first steps on the road of Faith. As he traces backward and forward the generations of the world, he makes the acquaintance of that which is no less than Eternal. As he meditates the course of outspreading matter and space, he recognizes that which is Infinite. As he tracks the restless energies of the Kosmos, he comes to know that which he cannot call less than Omnipotent. Through the multitudinous variety of the universe, he discerns the Unity on the axis of which all turns—

the single centre from which all radiates. In the contemplation of this stupendous power, the man of science is absorbed. He believes that all happiness depends upon the knowledge of it, and the conforming of men's lives to it. He recognizes himself as bound up with it, and is filled with inexpressible awe as, in his studies, he enters into its marvelous secrets. "It comes that," as Strauss says, "he demands for his Kosmos the same piety that the devout man of old demanded for his God." Thus Science imbues its devotees with the spirit of worship; leads them, if not to the inner, nevertheless to the outer court of Religion. Only one more step is needed—that from the force to the Cause; from the law to the Lawgiver—to bring them into the temple of God.

And this further step Science ought logically to take. The boast of Bacon that he had taken all knowledge as his province is the duty of Science To ignore the whole domain of spiritual truth is but half to perform its mission.

Religion has its facts as well as Science; the immaterial thought, the self-directing will, the sense of right and wrong, the consciousness of moral responsibility, these are facts as much as attraction of magnet or undulation of sound-wave. Sublime aspirations, immortal longings which protoplasm cannot account for; heroisms and self-sacrifices not to be explained on the principle of the greatest good of the greatest number; a current in human affairs that runs steadily toward the right, the true, and the good—these, also, are facts. A complete science ought to study these facts candidly, and draw from them their logical inductions—soul and God ; a complete science should take note, not only of the verifications of physical doctrines, in physical experience, but of these equally strong verifications in spiritual experience of spiritual truths. It should own the force not only of those native predispositions that assure us of Nature's constancy and Matter's indestructibility, but of those ineradicable convictions that asseverate the soul's immortality. It should recognize not only the questioning of the human mind for second causes, but its imperative demand for the First Cause. Does it become Science to exert itself so diligently merely to pass from effect to anterior effect, from one law to another law, only a little more simple, but never ask what is the prime power on which all depend—the Lawgiver behind all the laws ? Shall it trace with such painstaking assiduity every thread of the Kosmos, each hair-breadth of those exquisite webs of interacting laws, so harmoniously blended, so pervaded with the tokens of profoundest intelligence, and then, when we ask for the Weaver of this infinite marvel, the Reality behind this veil—tell us there is none—the *veil* is *all ?* No ! The true man of science must work with that conviction under which Whewell says he wrote his " Philosophy of the Inductive Sciences," " that no philosophy of the universe can satisfy the minds of thoughtful men which does not deal with such questions as inevitably force themselves upon our notice, respecting the Author and the object of the universe; and also under the conviction that every philosophy of the universe which has any consistency must suggest answers, at least, conjectural, to such questions. No Kosmos is complete from which the question of Deity is excluded; and all Kosmology has a side turned toward Theology."

It is through the mastering and manifestation of this *theological* side, this Godward face, that Science delivers to mankind its noblest message. That which makes Science something more than the gratification of an idle curiosity or a low-lived utilitarianism—that which gives to it in the thoughts of the higher-minded a sacred dignity—is the belief that by it we are daily making clearer and clearer the ways of that Infinite Power, the features of that Divine Image, which all things shadow forth.

Soon may that happy day—happy for both alike —dawn upon the world, when Religion and Science, recognizing the common ground on which they stand, the similar methods, objects, and results which characterize each, the need they stand in of each other, the one God of whom they both prophesy, shall cordially join hands in his service!

THE END.

www.ingramcontent.com/pod-product-compliance
Lightning Source LLC
Chambersburg PA
CBHW030116030726
47498CB00007B/2408